Alt-Finance

'Fascinating. Shows convincingly that Brexit was financed by hedge funds and alternative finance, and that their ultimate goal was to promote a new wave of financial deregulation and buy off our democratic institutions. A great piece of social sciences and a must-read.'

—Thomas Piketty, author of *Capital in the Twenty-First Century*

'Growing inequalities and processes of financialisation require much closer scrutiny of the social dynamics of capital accumulation and the new forms of political power that are accompanying it. This careful study does precisely that. A fresh and urgent agenda for social science research for years to come.'

—Johan Heilbron, Professor, Sociology of Education, Uppsala University

'A most remarkable foray into the radicalisation of the political order inherent in our contemporary financial condition: an order for which remaining pockets of liberal democracy are no longer of use.'

—Fabian Muniesa, Professor, École des Mines de Paris

'Marlène Benquet and Théo Bourgeron's provocative opus remarkably demonstrates how conflicts among different fractions of capital were the key drivers of UK's recent Eighteenth Brumaire: Brexit.'

—Olivier Godechot, author of *Wages, Bonuses and the Appropriation of Profit in the Financial Industry*

Alt-Finance

How the City of London Bought Democracy

Marlène Benquet and Théo Bourgeron

Translated by Meg Morley and Théo Bourgeron

First published as *La Finance autoritaire: Vers la fin du néolibéralisme*
by Raisons d'agir éditions 2021

First English language edition published 2022 by Pluto Press
New Wing, Somerset House, Strand, London WC2R 1LA
and Pluto Press Inc.
1930 Village Center Circle, Ste. 3-384, Las Vegas, NV 89134

www.plutobooks.com

British Library Cataloguing in Publication Data
A catalogue record for this book is available from the British Library

ISBN 978 0 7453 4758 5   Hardback
ISBN 978 0 7453 4685 4   Paperback
ISBN 978 0 7453 4760 8   PDF
ISBN 978 0 7453 4759 2   EPUB

This book is printed on paper suitable for recycling and made from fully
managed and sustained forest sources. Logging, pulping and manufacturing
processes are expected to conform to the environmental standards of the
country of origin.

Typeset by Stanford DTP Services, Northampton, England

Simultaneously printed in the United Kingdom and United States of America

Contents

List of Tables

quicker than the cycle of writing and publishing. We hope that the translation of this book will contribute to a better understanding of the new political regimes of accumulation whose emergence we are now witnessing.

Marlène Benquet and Théo Bourgeron
Paris and Cologne, 5 May 2022

Introduction

In the presidential election of 8 November 2016, the United States of America, the world's foremost economic and political power, was stunned by the surprise victory of Donald Trump, a newcomer to politics. The candidate Trump, less well known and less well funded than his opponent Hillary Clinton, had been treated as an outsider. When he won the election the press presented him as the spokesperson of voiceless people, of an ignored and demoted white middle-class in an increasingly inegalitarian country. It is no secret that Hillary Clinton received the support of some of the most emblematic representatives of the financial community, to the extent that the media ended up calling her the 'Wall Street candidate'. What is less well known, however, is that Donald Trump too benefited from the support of powerful billionaires in the financial sector, including Robert Mercer, founder of the quantitative trading hedge fund Renaissance Technologies; Doug Manchester, founder of the Manchester Financial Group; and Duke and Hannah Buchan, founders of the investment fund Hunter Global Investors. More recently enriched than the Wall Street institutions supporting Clinton, less visible and with no historical connections to government or public affairs, these billionaires involved in the most speculative forms of finance nonetheless managed to impose their candidate over the one preferred by the powerful traditional institutions of Wall Street. And this in turn allowed Trump to try to convert the United States to a political programme made up of a novel mix of authoritarianism, climate change denial, financial deregulation and the unconditional defence of capital and property against all forms of redistribution, however minimal.

On 28 October 2018 Jair Bolsonaro campaigned on a similar political programme to win the presidential election in Brazil. Bolsonaro, a former army captain, was a self-confessed admirer of the dictatorship period in his country and an outspoken denier of climate change. He had the support of the most reactionary forces in the Brazilian Parliament, including the BBB (Bible, beef, bullets) lobby, whose members represent the interests of evangelical churches, the agribusiness sector and the gun lobby. As with Trump, Bolsonaro's political programme combined authoritarianism with far-reaching economic deregulation. Twenty-four hours after having been elected, he decided by presidential decree to lower the minimum wage, to transfer authority for indigenous territories to the agriculture ministry (closely aligned with agribusiness) and to eliminate the ministry in charge of defending the rights of the LGBT community. His campaign was supported by broad segments of the business community. In July 2018, the president of the National Confederation for Industry (CNI), the Brazilian equivalent of the Confederation of British Industry (CBI), declared that the business community was not afraid of Bolsonaro's victory, saying that 'people want a president who will display his strength and his authority, but also be responsible'.[1] To secure the support of the most free-wheeling players in the Brazilian financial sector, Bolsonaro handed the economic aspects of his programme over to Paulo Guedes, known for having founded the libertarian think tank Instituto Millenium and the investment bank BTG Pactual. In the months following his election, Bolsonaro fulfilled several of his campaign promises, loosening the laws on gun ownership, introducing a sweeping reform of the pension system and launching the privatisation of most state-owned companies. These last two reforms had long been advocated by the libertarian Guedes, who was now minister of the economy.

On the morning of 24 June 2016, the United Kingdom discovered that 51.9 per cent of voters had voted to 'Leave' in answer to the question: 'Should the United Kingdom remain a member of the European Union or leave the European Union?' Thus began Brexit – a process that would culminate with the accession to power of a leader, Boris Johnson, and ministers known for their often authoritarian, climate-sceptical and pro-deregulation opinions. The result of the referendum came as a surprise, to put it mildly, to the government, the business community and the British population. On June 22, the day before the vote, the BBC and Sky News had broadcast the latest polls, all of which predicted a victory for 'Remain'. After a three-month campaign during which the two main parties, the most eminent members of the business community and the principal trade unions had all campaigned to persuade the British people to vote for Remain, this was an astonishing result. Representatives of the banking sector had staunchly supported Remain, as had the Chancellor of the Exchequer and the governor of the Bank of England. The City of London Corporation, the lobby of the London-based financial sector, had also put its political might behind the Remain vote. In April 2016, it had warned the British people that 'the City of London is the leading international financial centre in the world. It is the most cosmopolitan major business city in the world and [... a Leave vote would be] unwelcome and unhelpful.'

But at 6:07 am on 24 June, Boris Johnson made a speech to a jubilant crowd: 'My friends, I promised you: we are taking back control of our great country. I now proclaim Year One of an independent Britain!'[2] Two hours later the Conservative prime minister David Cameron, who had triggered the referendum but supported Remain, also made a statement, standing in front of 10 Downing Street and looking visibly shaken:

> I was absolutely clear about my belief that Britain is stronger, safer and better off inside the European Union, and I made clear the referendum was about this and this alone – not the future of any single politician, including myself … I will do everything I can as Prime Minister to steady the ship over the coming weeks and months, but I do not think it would be right for me to try to be the captain that steers our country to its next destination.

Nigel Farage, the leader of the Eurosceptic party UKIP, declared after the announcement of the referendum result: 'The EU is failing, the EU is dying. I hope we've knocked the first brick out of the wall.' Financial panic began on the night of 23 June, and accelerated apace as the British political landscape disintegrated. To reassure companies and calm the financial markets, Cameron announced that he would lower the corporate tax rate (from 20 per cent to 15 per cent) before leaving office, and the Bank of England declared that it was ready to inundate British financial markets with liquidities to 'support their functioning' in this challenging moment. But the harm had been done: the government had been defeated, and the City had been weakened.

How could such a thing occur? Tim Harford, a *Financial Times* columnist, wrote that 'if the City had had infinite powers, Brexit would not have occurred'. Does this mean that the most powerful financial sector in Europe did not have the means to make its voice heard on an issue that was so crucial for its own future? In the US presidential election, were Wall Street and the biggest US banks unable to secure victory for the candidate they seemed to have unanimously chosen? As happened in 2005 when the French and Dutch electorates voted against the European constitutional treaty, did the mechanisms that usually bind liberal democracies to the interests of the dominant economic sectors malfunction? In other words, were the Brexit referendum and the elections of Trump and Bolsonaro victories of the people against the elite and the financial sector?

We explore these questions by taking a closer look at the relationship between Brexit and the British financial sector. This closer look begins with the morning of 24 June 2016, when some dissonant details came to the fore. For instance, when making his victory speech at Westminster, UKIP leader Nigel Farage was not alone: he was flanked by two friends and political supporters, Arron Banks and Richard Tice. The two were not only supporters of Brexit, but also businessmen active in the financial sector – Banks owned a network of diverse companies, from retail insurance to offshore wealth management, and Tice was the CEO of a real estate investment fund. On this same morning, in a posh Mayfair house a few miles from Westminster, a BBC team captured the moment when a major British hedge fund manager, Crispin Odey, burst out in laughter while talking about the referendum result: 'I have had a good day!', he repeated with jubilation. Innocuous as they might seem, these two anecdotes suggest that behind the outspoken support of large City banks for Remain there lay a more complicated landscape. In the same way as the elections of Trump in the United States and Bolsonaro in Brazil were in fact supported by some fringes of the financial sector, it seems that British finance entertained a far more ambiguous relationship to Brexit and right-wing politics than has been commonly recognised. In this book we investigate how, behind the well-known pro-Remain institutions of the City of London, another more discreet set of London-based financial actors supported Brexit. We call these alternative financial actors 'alt-finance' in reference both to their investment strategies, which are often deemed 'alternative' by financial analysts themselves, and to their political support for new right-wing movements, labelled 'alt-right' in the US context.

Here our work diverges from the most common interpretations of Brexit. Whatever their political orientations, most analyses have interpreted Brexit as the consequence of people's anger against the European Union. The Eurosceptic right and far-right cheered the 'victory of ordinary people against the establishment', to quote Farage. Without underestimating the significance of xenophobic ideas in the outcome of the vote, some voices on the left also perceived the result as a first step towards the dismantling of the neoliberal order. Similar arguments have been developed to explain the election of Donald Trump. In 2016 Bill Clinton expounded that Trump's victory was due first and foremost to the mobilisation of 'angry white men' and other middle-class citizens who felt they had been socially demoted. Although the context was different in Brazil, where the Labour Party had been dominant from 2003 to 2016, a study by the World Inequality Lab attributed Bolsonaro's victory to the relative impoverishment of the Brazilian middle class. Despite being diverse and sometimes in contradiction, these views share a common analysis of political events as resulting from the (good and bad) reasoning and impulses of voters. In this discourse, the Leave, Trump and Bolsonaro votes had in common their social heterogeneity, in that they united segments of the bourgeoisie with segments of the working class. This has led some analysts to interpret them as 'electoral insurgencies' of the neglected countryside and formerly industrial regions against the urban establishment that rules the economy.[3] These votes are described as the political expression of working- and middle-class voters' resentment against the globalisation process, which has placed them in competition with workers in low- and middle-income countries and threatens to dispossess them of what little wealth they have. The votes are taken to display a deep anger against political systems, most prominently in the UK and the US, and more broadly against the contemporary world order, in which traditional politics offer no alternative to neoliberalism.

These interpretations are useful in understanding the mindset of voters, but they beg the crucial question of how the economic interests of the dominant classes came into play in these campaigns. They also contribute to an overly idealistic understanding of electoral processes – suggesting that the vote is essentially a matter of ideas and dominant opinions. They perceive an election as a vast debate that takes place in a democratic arena spanning television networks, newspapers, social media and exchanges between citizens wherever they may be. Following this debate, voters, informed by discussion of the campaign arguments, cast ballots to choose the political vision or programme that has gained their support. The main threat to such a democratic debate lies in the corruption of this democratic arena through argumentative demagogy and other electoral manipulations. As with the elections of Trump and Bolsonaro, many researchers have tried to explain the outcome of the Brexit referendum by highlighting the effects of the fake news that proliferated during the campaign. Writing in the *New York Times*, political economist Will Davies denounced the way fake news considerably affected the fair expression of ideas during the American presidential campaign.[4] And indeed, the Leave vote and the Trump victory led to inquiries into the role of the British company Cambridge Analytica, which was accused of distorting the campaigns by using the personal social media data of British and American citizens to influence the votes. By reducing these political events to the result of electoral manipulations, however, these interpretations miss structural factors. They leave out the power relationships among social groups, including the business community, that have emerged in a spectacular way since 2016 and that have contributed to the change in political regime under way in Europe and the rest of the world.

In this book, we focus on the ongoing shift from the neoliberal political regime of accumulation towards what we call the new libertarian-authoritarian regime. Since the 1970s the neoliberal regime has opened up new sources of profit by drawing large swathes of social life into financial markets. The neoliberalism of Western countries has been accompanied by free-market democratic institutions that channel popular discontent cheaply and without threatening capitalist accumulation. These institutions constitute what we call in this work the 'neoliberal political regime of accumulation'. On the international scale the European Union has become one of the flagship institutions of neoliberalism. Its treaties transfer numerous fields of social organisation in its member states to market actors, especially financial markets. In this context, the Brexit vote appeared to cut the United Kingdom loose from the flagship vessel of the neoliberal political regime of accumulation. The election of Donald Trump had a similar effect: it led the United States to break with the World Trade Organization, another emblematic international institution of the neoliberal regime. As we see here, neoliberal institutions are dying.

Should we rejoice? Probably not. The British exit from the European Union was certainly a step away from neoliberalism and towards something else. However, this step was taken not by progressive forces seeking to set up more egalitarian institutions, but by rising capitalist forces eager to assert their domination within a new accumulation regime. The idea that new capitalist forces might coalesce to attack neoliberal institutions and create a more authoritarian accumulation regime has been hotly disputed in recent years. David Harvey, for instance, has refuted the contention that events such as the election of Donald Trump and the Brexit referendum are anything other than neoliberal business-as-usual.[5] In his perspective, neoliberalism is essentially a way for 'the dominant classes to reassert their domination' and accumulation regimes can change their institutions without ceasing to be fundamentally neoliberal. Other observers, however, consider neoliberalism to be embodied in the set of institutions through which it was built up over decades, and see recent events as marking the potential emergence of a 'post-neoliberal' order.[6] Quinn Slobodian highlights 'the backlash from above' by which the corporate class used the Trump election to seize power in the United States. In cogent books and articles, he has described the corporate forces that supported the Trump administration's opposition to the World Trade Organization, designated as the cause of 'neoliberal globalisation'.[7] McKenzie Wark has also recently questioned whether the new dominant classes of the technological age are still aligned with neoliberal capitalism, and wonders whether they are looking for another accumulation regime that would allow them to expand their profits.[8]

This book describes the advent of this new political regime of accumulation that is replacing the declining neoliberal regime in the United Kingdom, the United States and Brazil. We give the new regime a name – the libertarian-authoritarian regime. Libertarianism rests on the radical defence of private property, posited as the main (and often sole) rule of social organisation, without regard for its collective consequences. It limits the role of the state, including in its sovereign functions. We will see that while the regime that is emerging in the UK, the US and Brazil is libertarian on economic issues, it is authoritarian on political issues. As this regime is hostile to all redistribution of wealth, it uses repression of social movements, curtailment of civil liberties and restriction of public demonstrations and speeches as the main way to enforce social order. In this book we describe how and why some segments of the business community supported Brexit, and how Brexit was the first significant instance of a country shifting from the neoliberal to the libertarian-authoritarian political regime of accumulation.[9] In our exploration we look at elections from the angle of their funding rather than the psychology of electorates.

We aim to show that Brexit was the consequence of an economic opposition between two factions of the British financial sector that became an institutional and political conflict. Like the United States and, to a lesser extent, Brazil, the United Kingdom is on the cutting edge of financialisation. A large proportion of its national profit is concentrated in financial corporations and in the considerable fortunes amassed by the tycoons of this sector. In addition to the historical financial sector, which we call 'first-wave' finance (large banks, insurance companies, institutional investors), whose mode of accumulation relies mostly on stock markets, a new front of financialisation has developed in recent decades in the United Kingdom. We designate this alternative financial sector as 'second-wave' finance. It operates at the least regulated margins of the financial sector (including private equity funds, hedge funds and real estate funds) via over-the-counter transactions involving assets that were until recently unavailable to financial speculation.[10] These groups of financiers have distinct economic interests. Above all, they now find themselves competing with each other to negotiate the political regime of accumulation that will best defend their right to accumulate capital and wealth. Although the European Union has fuelled the development of the European financial sector over the past four decades, it now seems that finance may have to jettison this institutional architecture if it wants to continue to expand. This is the bet that second-wave financial players make when they seek to replace the institutions of neoliberalism with a new regime based on a novel mix of economic libertarianism and political authoritarianism – a regime negotiated at the national scale and favourable to their interests. In this book we study the history of support for and opposition to Brexit within the British financial sector during the referendum campaign and then during the Brexit negotiations. Through these examples we show the role that second-wave finance played in undermining the established neoliberal institutions and in promoting a political regime that espouses radically reactionary views on democracy, the environment and society as a whole.

We are going to follow the money in order to understand Brexit not in the light of the issues that motivated voters, but through the flows of cold hard cash that allowed this event to happen.[11] We examine this process from the top, from the viewpoint of those who are accustomed to paying to secure laws that will protect their private interests.[12] We approach Brexit as the project of a rising faction of the financial sector that is in competition with other parts of the business community and traditional finance. This faction is characterised by its own mode of financial accumulation and is determined to expand its perspectives for enrichment. We set the story of Brexit in the arena of the struggles within the financial sector, and in the history of political accumulation regimes over the past four decades, with a view to understanding why it happened and who decided to pay to make it happen.[13]

1

The Big Money Behind Brexit

The unforeseen outcome of the referendum weakened the largest financial centre in Europe. Brexit seemed to be quite a bad deal for the City. The most visible representatives of the City had made it abundantly clear during the campaign that they did not want Brexit, and their disappointment when the results were announced bore witness to their sincerity. How could such a powerful sector fail to prevent the referendum from taking place, and further fail to influence its outcome?

A referendum held against the will of the financial sector?

After months of dithering, David Cameron, the prime minister, proclaimed on 20 February 2016 that a referendum on the membership of the United Kingdom in the European Union would take place on 23 June 2016. Despite being aware that such an announcement was looming, this came as a shock for the main representatives of the industrial and financial business communities. They had extensively made public that they were against Brexit, and were opposed to a referendum on it. The British Bankers' Association, the lobbying group of the banking sector, stated that 'the banking sector unequivocally [wants] to maintain the current level of full access to the European Union market, to ensure that businesses and individuals across the European Union can still be served by London-based banks'. A few days later, 198 business leaders, representing some of the largest companies in the UK (including Asda, BT, Marks & Spencer and Vodafone) with 1.2 million employees in all, published in *The Times* a column warning British voters of the dangers of Brexit. What was wrong with the government? Why would it take the risk of submitting such a sensitive question for the business community to a popular vote? Of course, Cameron was quick to declare that 'the United Kingdom will be stronger, safer and better off by remaining as a member of a reformed EU', explicitly campaigning in favour of the Remain side. But the outcome of a referendum is always uncertain – especially a referendum on the European Union. In 2005 the proposed European constitutional treaty had spurred a wave of referendums across Europe, and French voters unexpectedly torpedoed the whole project by voting against it, quickly followed by the Dutch. European governments learned from their mistakes, and in 2008 the ratification process of the Lisbon treaty was conducted exclusively through much safer parliamentary procedures. (The Irish government alone made the mistake of submitting the treaty to a referendum. Irish voters rejected the Lisbon treaty in June 2008 and the government had great difficulty explaining why they needed a second referendum in October 2009 to ultimately overturn the first referendum and approve the treaty.) Did this mean that the British government had suddenly broken with the cosy interdependency it had maintained with its business community for decades? Unless one naively believes that the state acts in an autonomous and neutral way, independent of the economic lobbies that dominate its territory, and that public action is exclusively determined by party politics and the personal opinions of the highest members of government, it is hard to understand what lay behind the decision of the prime minister. Cameron had the support of many representatives of the industrial and financial sectors when he was elected; what led him to endanger one of the pillars of the institutional arrangement that guaranteed the prosperity of these sectors?

Let us first outline the events that led to the referendum and the ultimate Brexit victory. Only after that will we be able to re-read this political chronicle through more materialist lenses and grasp its underlying meaning. The referendum came as the culmination of a long story. As early as 2007, Cameron, then leader of the Conservative Party, had promised to organise a referendum on the Lisbon treaty if his party won the general election in 2010. The Tories did win, but they entered into a coalition with the pro-European Liberal Democrats, and prudently did not mention the promise again. Three years later, in 2013, as his party was going through a new period of electoral uncertainty, Cameron again raised the prospect of a referendum:

> For us, the European Union is a means to an end – prosperity, stability, the anchor of freedom and democracy both within Europe and beyond her shores [...] I never want us to pull up the drawbridge and retreat from the world. I am not a British isolationist [...] The next Conservative manifesto in 2015 will ask for a mandate from the British people for a Conservative government to negotiate a new settlement with our European partners in the next parliament. It will be a relationship with the single market at its heart. And when we have negotiated that new settlement, we will give the British people a referendum with a very simple in or out choice. To stay in the EU on these new terms or come out altogether.

His proposal to hold a referendum on the issue was immediately saluted by political organisations across the board, from UKIP, the British National Party and the Northern Irish Democratic Unionist Party (DUP) on the right, to the Greens and the Respect Party on the left. The Labour Party leader Ed Miliband announced that Labour was opposed to such a referendum, unless the European Union enacted new transfers of competencies (it did not).

For what reason or reasons did Cameron suddenly decide to go to the headquarters of the Bloomberg financial information network in the United States and declare, on 23 January 2013, that he was determined to organise a referendum on UK membership in the European Union if the Tory Party won the next general election? After three years in power, Cameron was in trouble. The general election in 2010 had led to a hung Parliament, leading the Tories to join with the Liberal Democrats to form the first coalition government the country had known since 1945. In addition, the next general election was scheduled to take place in two years' time, in 2015, and the Labour Party, led by Ed Miliband, was ahead in the opinion polls. With Eurosceptic voices gaining strength within the Conservative Party, the prime minister found himself between a rock and a hard place. The euro crisis and the conspicuous alignment of German and French policies towards an increasingly federalist agenda were making Conservatives fearful of potential coming transfers of sovereignty. This was especially worrying to Cameron, given that an increasing portion of his own electorate was attracted to the Eurosceptic UKIP stance. Formed in 1993, just after the Maastricht treaty, this party was led by Nigel Farage, a former London Metals Exchange broker turned political leader, who had become highly visible in the period from 2010 to 2014. UKIP got 3 per cent of the vote in the 2010 general election and 27.5 per cent of the vote in the 2014 European elections, helped by the centrist position of the Conservative/Lib-Dem coalition and benefiting from the controversial behaviour of the UKIP leader. (One egregious incident occurred at the European Parliament session of February 2010, when Farage insulted the president of the

European Council, Herman Van Rompuy, telling him that he had 'all the charisma of a damp rag and the appearance of a low-grade bank clerk' and accusing him of being the 'quiet assassin of European democracy and of European nation states'.)

In deciding to make the Brexit referendum his signature issue for the coming general election, Cameron's intention was to unite the Conservative electorate. But in 2014 this strategy had not borne fruit. Far from being weakened, UKIP was doing better than ever. Cameron's promise gave legitimacy to organisations that had been calling for a referendum for decades, drawing them out of their former political marginality. When UKIP won 27.5 per cent of votes in the UK European elections on 25 May 2014 – a higher vote share than either Labour or the Conservatives – *The Times* saw fit to designate Nigel Farage as the 2014 'Briton of the year'.

Distasteful to significant parts of the British business community, but quite popular with the Conservative electorate, the referendum promise was intended to ensure Cameron's victory in the 2015 general election. But it also played another role. The prime minister was hoping to put an end to the constantly simmering rejection of the EU that was crippling his party, and to definitively establish the legitimacy of the European project in the UK. This was because, in 2013, and later in 2014 and 2015, Cameron did not believe that Brexit would prevail. When Herman Van Rompuy visited him at the Chequers residence, Cameron told him that 'once we have won the referendum, we'll have settled the European issue in the United Kingdom for at least two decades'. He had no doubt that his referendum promise would weaken UKIP at the next general election, and that the Brexit side, without support from any major party, would lose the referendum. Similarly, Donald Tusk, who replaced Van Rompuy as president of the European Council, reported that he had asked Cameron about

Brexit: 'I asked David Cameron, why did you decide on this referendum [...] it's so dangerous, so stupid even [...] and he told me that the only reason was his own decision, but he had felt really safe, because he had thought that there was no risk involved, because his coalition partner, the Liberals, would block this idea of a referendum.'[1]

To achieve these two objectives – winning the 2015 general election by winning back the Eurosceptic electorate of UKIP, and legitimating UK membership in the EU through a referendum a few months later – Cameron's strategy was simple. He intended to lead a critical campaign against the European Union during the general election, and then, once re-elected, negotiate a new membership agreement with the EU to justify his support for the Remain vote during the Brexit referendum.

He put this political tactic to work starting in March 2014, one year before the general election that would return him to office. In a manifesto published that year, he outlined the association agreement between the UK and the EU that he intended to negotiate: there would be no fundamental change to the European treaties, but the British Parliament would have greater control over the implementation of European decisions, British companies would be subject to less so-called 'EU red tape', and talks to obtain an EU–US free trade agreement would proceed at a faster pace. He assumed that the new European Commission due to be elected at that time would be in favour of strengthening the power of member states in the EU. But on 27 June 2014 he had his first setback. Despite all Cameron's efforts to block his nomination, Jean-Claude Juncker, a former prime minister of Luxembourg and partisan of a federal European Union, was elected to the presidency of the European Commission. 'This is a serious mistake', Cameron warned. 'Jean-Claude Juncker has been at the heart of the project to increase the power of Brussels and reduce the power of nation states for his entire working life.'[2]

However, on a purely electoral level, Cameron's strategy seemed to work. In the 2015 general election he garnered an unexpected win. With 37 per cent of the votes, the Tories had achieved their most striking victory since the election of Margaret Thatcher. Both Labour and the Liberal Democrats were crushed. Labour's leader Ed Miliband resigned, and Cameron confirmed that he would hold a referendum the following year. On 27 May 2015, in a speech Cameron had drafted for her, Queen Elizabeth II announced that 'early legislation will be introduced to provide for an in-out referendum on membership of the European Union before the end of 2017'. The new temporary Labour leader, Harriet Harman, finally endorsed the plan for such a referendum. Now that his criticism aimed at the European Union had enabled Cameron to unite his camp and win the election, he needed to campaign *in favour* of the European Union, so that UK membership in the EU would be legitimated by a vote in favour of Remain. How could he achieve this? By staging tough negotiations for a new membership agreement for the UK, to convince Eurosceptic Conservative voters that the European Union of the mid-2010s was not the European Union of the 2000s and that, even if they had thought it in the British interest to leave the EU before, it was now in their interest to remain within this new EU.

It took one year for Cameron to perform this rhetorical sleight-of-hand. On 10 November 2015, he sent a letter presenting very general requests to the president of the European Council. Three months later, he went to Brussels in person to begin talks on a new agreement. In his own words, 'This will be difficult. I will be battling for Britain.'[3] Along with less substantial demands, the prime minister asked that the UK be exempted from the principle of free circulation of people (and workers). He also wanted the UK to be able to refuse social benefits to migrants from the continent for seven years after their arrival in the country. But it became clear that he had overestimated the effects the threat of a referendum would have on his negotiations with other European member states. In February 2016, most European leaders were sceptical that the Leave side could win and therefore did not see any real reason to accommodate British requests. After fruitless negotiations, the German Chancellor Angela Merkel agreed at the last minute to the demand that the UK be authorised to limit the benefits of migrants recently arrived in the country from the European continent. This very modest victory was nevertheless considered enough. Cameron saved appearances and could justify to the British people his active campaign in favour of Remain.

On 19 February 2016, he posted a tweet announcing that he had negotiated a deal to give the United Kingdom 'special status' in the EU. The next day, back in London, he announced in a serious but satisfied tone that the referendum would take place on 23 June 2016, and called for a vote in favour of the UK remaining a member of the European Union, in the name of this new agreement that gave the British people 'the best of the two worlds'.

When reading this chronicle, we see the limits of a political analysis that perceives the state as no more than an instrument of the dominant class. Inspired by agonistic views of society, in these approaches the action of governments is by definition taken to foster the interests of the dominant class. The state does not aim to subsume private interests to the general interest; on the contrary, it aims to augment the advantages that the most powerful enjoy in order to maximise their well-being. The state is then described as lacking the autonomy to pursue its own objectives. The relations of the state with the dominant segments of society can only be relations of subordination. The similar social background and careers of the power elite in place in public administration and in the private sector are advanced as evidence of this subordination.[4] Subordination is maintained by the effectiveness of lobbies funded by the dominant classes,[5] and by the structural power possessed by dominant groups.[6] In this view, the law always benefits the powerful, who do not even need to produce any proof of their might. These analyses generally rest on the conception of the state as the 'guardian of the interests of the economic elite', whose real mission is 'to ensure the perpetuation of its domination'.[7] Being merely an instrument in the hands of the powerful, the subjugation of the state knows no bounds.

These analyses omit another set of constraints that weigh on the action of the state; namely, the management of populations. The manipulation of the state by the dominant classes is limited by their dependency on other social groups. For instance, it is limited by the need of dominant classes to ensure that state institutions are not overthrown by social unrest. State authorities have to please what, in the 1920s, Antonio Gramsci named 'civil society', in order to ensure that subordinated social groups do not use their power of disturbance against the elite. State action in any given period of history depends on how it resolves the conflict between these two orders of dependency: dependency on the dominant classes, whose power is institutionalised by the state, and dependency on civil society, from which the state draws its legitimacy. The state is the institutional representation of the relationship between dominant and dominated groups;[8] it acts in a context of double dependency on the dominant classes and on the population that it governs.

In this respect, David Cameron displayed truly *political* reasoning in the mid-2010s. Even though the British business community was worried that the Brexit referendum would give voters the opportunity to make a choice that would be contrary to business interests, now and again the government had to show voters that it represented them. Cameron took a risk with the referendum – a risk not only for him, but also for the dominant classes that had supported him since he was first elected in 2010. He took this risk to preserve his government's legitimacy, that is to say to safeguard the fiction of a government that would express the people's will. To maintain this precarious balance, what steps did the British business community take to ensure that the dependency of the state on the will of the people would not produce an outcome that would threaten its economic interests?

The referendum campaign began unofficially in October 2015. Europhiles flocked together to form the Britain Stronger in Europe group, presided by Stuart Rose, a Conservative peer and former chairman of Marks & Spencer. This group was supported by three ex-prime ministers, Tony Blair and Gordon Brown of the Labour Party, and John Major from the Conservative Party. The group was constituted before the official start of the referendum campaign, so that it could begin early on persuading electors to vote for Remain, but also so that it could spend money before the Electoral Commission had begun to register accounts of campaign expenses. Campaign groups could spend no more than £7 million during the four months of the official referendum campaign. On the Leave side, two campaign groups emerged in the same period. Vote Leave Ltd described itself as nonpartisan and included Conservatives, Eurosceptic Labour representatives and even UKIP supporters. Vote Leave Ltd ostentatiously staged its nonpartisan nature by designating three treasurers representing each of these political streams, although Eurosceptic Conservatives were in fact dominant within the group. Its main strategist was Dominic Cummings, who had spent most of his career advising Conservative leaders and was strongly critical of UKIP. Vote Leave Ltd was the author of the campaign slogan suggesting that Brexit would allow the UK to redirect its EU contribution to the National Health Service

(NHS), in the amount of £350 million a week. The second group, Leave.EU, was led mostly by UKIP figures, among whom were Nigel Farage and Arron Banks, a businessman who had been a major donor to the Conservative Party before switching his allegiance to UKIP. Leave.EU targeted mostly UKIP and dissatisfied Labour voters, and built its campaign around migration issues. On 13 April 2016, the Electoral Commission announced that the Vote Leave Ltd group had been chosen to lead the official campaign in favour of Leave, and Britain Stronger in Europe for the Remain side. The latter renamed itself as 'The In Campaign'.

Most trade unions and business federations supported the Remain campaign. Trade unions underscored how important EU membership was for improving labour regulations in Europe and in the UK. UNITE and Unison, two of the main British trade unions, jointly published an open letter informing their members that 'after much debate and deliberation we believe that the social and cultural benefits of remaining in the EU far outweigh any advantages of leaving'.[9] As for business organisations, John Cridland, the head of CBI, the largest British business federation, had already denounced the dangers of Brexit in the *Observer* in 2014: 'A large majority of CBI businesses of all sizes are clear: the UK is best served inside a reformed EU, rather than outside with no influence.'[10] Multinational companies based in the UK also went public on their support for Remain. The Institute of Directors (IOD), another business group, polled its roughly 1,000 members and found that 64 per cent thought that getting out of the EU would endanger their activity. According to CBI, the British economy stood to lose up to £100 billion and 1 million jobs by 2020 in the event of Brexit.

But what about finance? After all, the finance sector is one of the most powerful economic sectors in the UK and is known to exert a strong influence on British politics. As the financial capital of Europe, the British financial sector represents 7 per cent of the country's GDP, 25 per cent of corporate tax revenue, and 1.1 million jobs (over 2 million if indirect employment is included). If one listened to the media, read the professional newspapers and followed the statements of the chairmen of the main British financial institutions, it seemed that the financial community was almost unanimously in favour of the Remain side. Even before the date of the referendum was announced, Mark Carney, the governor of the Bank of England, expressed deep concerns about the consequences of Brexit for the British financial sector. Carney's worries were echoed by George Osborne, the Chancellor of the Exchequer.

The support of the City for staying in the EU was not surprising. It endorsed two decades of European regulations that had built a legal arrangement under which the City captured a large share of the financial surplus generated in the EU. Brexit would weaken the dominant City institutions in two main ways. For a start, they would risk losing all or some of the advantages of the European financial passport.[11] This provision allowed financial institutions accredited in one EU country to practise in all other EU states. Many US corporations (Bank of America, JPMorgan Chase, Citigroup) as well as Swiss and Japanese firms had located their headquarters in London in order to access the European market. Should London-based headquarters lose their European status and passports, these firms would be tempted to relocate and seek accreditation in another EU country. This was particularly significant given that fully one half of the 12,700 financial institutions established in London were European headquarters of foreign corporations. The CEO of Morgan Stanley, which employed 16,000 people in the UK at the time, warned that between 1,000 and 4,000 jobs could be relocated from the UK to the EU in the event of Brexit. The British bank HSBC also acknowledged that it might relocate some 1,000 jobs to Paris to keep its European passport if Brexit took place. Deutsche Bank, which employed 9,000 people in London, likewise announced it would repatriate some of its staff to Frankfurt in the event of Brexit. Following these statements, alarming studies were compiled on the cost of a Leave victory. PricewaterhouseCoopers (PwC) estimated that the British financial sector would lose between 70,000 and 100,000 jobs by 2020 in the event of Brexit. Beyond jobs, it was also feared that Brexit would have a high cost in terms of financial infrastructure. The City played a central role in euro clearing, that is to say the clearing of euro-denominated transactions, through the London Clearing House (LCH) Clearnet, the largest European compensation house.[12] Frankfurt, home to Clearnet's competitor Eurex, had already attempted in 2011 to bring all euro clearing to Frankfurt, arguing that it was necessary to clear euro-denominated transactions within the eurozone (of which the UK was not part) to ensure the financial stability of the monetary area. However, the European Court of Justice had opposed this move, arguing that the UK was a European member state. Brexit would clearly give Eurex a stronger hand in asking for euro-denominated transaction clearing to be relocated. In the event of Brexit, the UK would also lose the European Banking Authority, created in 2010 to oversee the European financial supervision network. The chief economist of the private bank Edmond de Rothschild predicted that, all in all, Brexit would likely cause the transfer of €700 billion in financial revenues from London to the European Union.

It seemed that it was entirely against the interests of the financial sector to lose its access to the European market. Throughout the 1990s and 2000s the European Union had been a favourable place for London finance. Legally, the EU never questioned the central financial role of the City. Politically, in the 1990s the EU went down the path of financial deregulation, reproducing at the European scale the British financial big bang of the 1980s. Ideologically, the EU played a useful role, bearing responsibility before the people of Europe for unpopular measures favourable to financial accumulation. In short, the European Union played a game that benefited the financial sector, and the City of London seemed to have good reasons not to leave it.

Despite all this support, Leave prevailed. This came as a shock. One week before the referendum, 120 financial executives had gathered at a meeting called by the Swiss asset manager Gam in London: 72 per cent of those in attendance were betting on Remain. Almost immediately after the announcement of the referendum result a press release was sent to the main financial news agencies by the governors of the Bank of England, the European Central Bank, the United States Federal Reserve Bank and the Bank of Japan. After huddling during the night for a call, the central bankers stated that 'they would pursue relentlessly their responsibility for monetary and financial stability' in the course of the Brexit process. The strong intentions of this statement were not enough to calm the rising panic in the financial sector. Rating agencies Standard & Poor's (S&P) and Fitch immediately downgraded the rating of the British long-term sovereign debt, from AAA to AA with a negative outlook. The pound sterling fell to its lowest parity with the dollar since 1985. The FTSE 100 index lost 7 per cent of its value at the opening of the London Stock Exchange. The broker Aurel BGC published a note advising that 'the financial sector should expect a very difficult session, especially for banks, that had recently bounced back following the hopes of a Remain victory'. The chief strategist of BlackRock Investment Institute, Isabelle Mateos y Lago, confirmed that 'Brexit has created an uncertainty shock, markets were not prepared to deal with it'.[13] To face the coming political turmoil, Goldman Sachs hired former European Commission president José Manuel Barroso to help the firm handle the consequences of the decision for its UK and European operations. In July 2016, most of the financial institutions mentioned here were struggling to adapt to Brexit, and it was hard to imagine how this situation could turn into a good deal for the sector.

Told in this way, Brexit looks like a story of poor tactical judgement, the result of the misguided manoeuvring of a political leader who took reckless risks to ensure his own re-election – in short, the unfortunate defeat of a demagogue, caught in his own trap. It might be possible to conclude that in this case 10 Downing Street paid heed to other forces, i.e. the electorate, and did not merely bow to the interests of City financial players. But British politics usually hews to a higher categorial imperative – that of enforcing the capitalist economic order.[14] The divergence between this imperative and the actual fact of Brexit calls for deeper examination. And indeed, the story as we have told it so far omits some lesser-known circumstances and events of the mid-2010s. Despite appearances, the financial sector did not rise unanimously against the risk of the UK seceding from the EU. Looking beyond the official statements and public positions to examine the flow of funding behind the referendum campaign, it becomes apparent that some financial actors encouraged Brexit – and, given the amounts at stake, they probably had good economic reasons for doing so. Behind the political event of Brexit, there lies an economic and financial rationale.

A tale of two Cities

The highly vocal and visible campaign led by City corporations in favour of Remain seems to have prevented most observers from seeing the positions taken by various other parts of the financial sector during the referendum. Indeed, there was another campaign, more discreet but nonetheless massive, organised and funded by financiers who wanted the UK to leave the European Union. It is easy to follow the tracks of this other campaign in the public data of the Electoral Commission.

How the funding of referendums works in the UK

The Electoral Commission is an independent body that supervises elections and regulates political funding in the UK. Its mandate was defined by the Political Parties, Elections and Referendums Act (PPERA, 2000). Before a referendum vote, the Electoral Commission designates a so-called campaign leader ('designated organisations') for each side of the debate. For the Brexit referendum, on 13 April 2016 the Commission designated The In Campaign (formerly Britain Stronger in Europe) as the leader of the Remain campaign, and Vote Leave Ltd as the leader of the Leave side. Other campaigning groups ('permitted participants') in referendums have to register with the Electoral Commission, but they are regulated by a different set of accounting rules from those that apply to the two lead groups. In the course of a campaign, the Commission publishes information on the donations that each group receives and the amount of money they spend.

For the purposes of the Commission, a referendum campaign takes place in two periods: an unofficial and unregulated pre-campaign period, followed by the official campaign. For the Brexit referendum the official campaign period ran from 15 April to 23 June 2016. During the official period, expenditures by the two lead groups are limited to £7 million, and the expenditures of the other participating groups are limited to £700,000 per group. Under the PPERA act the Commission grants up to £600,000 in subsidies to each of the two lead groups. The two groups are also allowed to send out one item of communication by post to all voters free of charge, and are entitled to free campaign broadcasts on UK television networks. The electoral law is based on the principle of equal opportunity, and the monitoring of expenditures is a key part of this. The law stipulates that the different campaign groups shall not cooperate with each other, unless they submit joint accounts for their spending (meaning their expenditures come under a single cap). This theoretically limits expenditures to ensure that neither side can 'buy' the election.

In the Brexit referendum, however, the functioning of the Electoral Commission was criticised after the vote. On 17 May 2017, the *Guardian* revealed the existence of a confidential agreement between the pro-Brexit campaign and Robert Mercer, a US billionaire and founder of a hedge fund called Renaissance Technologies, and one of his close associates, Steve Bannon, a contributor to Donald Trump's presidential election campaign. The newspaper reported that the Leave campaign had been assisted by a data mining company called Cambridge Analytica, which had provided services that were not declared as official donations to a campaign group. It also discovered that Cambridge Analytica was owned by AggregateIQ, whose main shareholder was Robert Mercer. The subsequent inquiry into the electoral funding of the referendum could not require AggregateIQ to answer its questions, as the company was located outside of British jurisdiction. The inquiry panel nonetheless concluded that it 'was satisfied beyond reasonable doubt' that these companies had unlawfully contributed to the Leave campaign. Cambridge Analytica was also accused of having used for political ends – i.e. the promotion of the Leave campaign – the personal data of millions of Facebook users that it had collected without their consent. In July 2018, the Electoral Commission decided to sanction the leading Leave campaign group, Vote Leave Ltd, for not having prevented this fraud. The group was fined for infraction of the electoral law. Despite the Electoral Commission's regulations and judicial action, foreign billionaires seem to have funded and influenced the Brexit referendum. Fraudulent electoral funding of course affects the accuracy of the funding records that we examine in this book. But since fraudulent funding was provided to the Leave campaign by billionaire hedge fund managers, this only bolsters our argument rather than undermining it.

The Electoral Commission identified all the donations received by all the campaign groups, both the lead groups (Vote Leave Ltd and The In Campaign) and other participating groups (including Leave.EU and a host of others). Donations were recorded during five distinct periods: pre-poll 1 during which donations and expenses were not capped, from 1 February to 21 April 2016, before the start of the official campaign; pre-poll 2, from 22 April to 12 May 2016; pre-poll 3, from 13 May to 9 June 2016; and pre-poll 4, from 10 to 22 June 2016. During pre-poll periods 2 to 4, donations remained uncapped, but expenditure was limited to £7 million for the lead groups and £700,000 for other participating groups. Our study integrates the donations recorded over the five periods considered by the Electoral Commission. The database we have compiled using the Electoral Commission data includes 349 donations from 313 distinct donors (some donors made several donations, either to the same group or to other campaign groups). These donations came from companies, individuals, trade unions, not-for-profit groups and public authorities. For each donation, the data reported by the Commission include the amount of the donation, the recipient, the date of the donation, the date of the receipt and the name and status of the donor. We added four additional variables: the economic activity sector from which the donation originated (e.g. construction, banking); whether this economic sector is part of the financial sector or not; and, for donations from individuals or companies operating in the financial sector, the nature of the financial activity (e.g. hedge fund, private equity fund, insurance brokerage) and the mode of accumulation that characterises this activity. These last two variables are described in greater detail below.

The data recorded by the Electoral Commission show the significant stakes of the Brexit referendum for corporations and wealthy individuals in the UK: they spent £33 million during the five months of the official campaign in their attempt to influence the outcome of the vote (Table 1).

Table 1   Total Donations Received in Each Period

Period of receipt of donations	Donations (in GBP)	Donations (in percentage of total donations)
From 1 February to 21 April 2016	15,522,135.90	47%
From 22 April to 12 May 2016	5,529,745.16	17%
From 13 May to 9 June 2016	7,084,911.67	21%
From 10 to 22 June 2016	4,918,092.60	15%
Total donations	33,054,885.33	

Donors gave a lot of money, and they gave it early, both to boost the prospect of victory for the side they had chosen, and to avoid the cap on expenditures in effect during the official campaign period. Nearly half of all donations were made before the beginning of the official campaign. The remaining donations came in at a regular pace during the official period. The Leave and Remain both sides received significant shares of these donations, with a sizeable advance for the Leave campaign (Table 2).

Table 2 Donations Received by Each Campaign

Campaign	Donations received (GBP)
Leave campaign	17,984,329.52
Remain campaign	15,070,555.81
Total	33,054,885.33

The Leave campaign received 54 per cent of all referendum donations, that is to say it had £2.9 million more than the Remain side to influence the referendum outcome. The timing of donations also differed between the two campaign groups (Table 3).

Table 3 Donations Received in Each Period by Each Campaign

Period of receipt of donations	Donations (in percentage of the total received by each campaign)
From 1 February to 21 April 2016	
Leave campaign	44.6%
Remain campaign	49.7%
From 22 April to 12 May 2016	
Leave campaign	22.0%
Remain campaign	10.4%
From 13 May to 9 June 2016	
Leave campaign	22.0%
Remain campaign	20.8%
From 10 June to 22 June 2016	
Leave campaign	11.3%
Remain campaign	19.1%

Overall, Remain groups received more funds before the official campaign and at the end of the official campaign. Leave groups received almost half of their funding during the first six weeks of the official campaign, that is to say when the Remain campaign received the least funding. Remain had money to spend before the beginning of the official campaign and at the end of it, whereas Leave had most of its money to spend at the beginning of the official campaign.

Let us now have a look at where the donations came from.

Table 4   Breakdown of Donations Received by Each Campaign

	Donations received (in GBP and in percentage of the total received by each campaign)
Leave campaign	17,984,329.52
Industrial sectors (secondary and tertiary)	43.3%
Financial sector	56.7%
Remain campaign	15,070,555.81
Industrial sectors (secondary and tertiary)	64.3%
Financial sector	35.7%

Over half (almost 57 per cent) of the money donated to the Leave campaign came from the financial sector, while that sector contributed only 36 per cent of the money donated to the Remain side. This distribution is a first surprise. The campaign most funded by the financial sector was not the one that people commonly think. This table overturns the assumption that the financial sector supported remaining in the European Union, while domestic industrial interests supported leaving. The funding figures show exactly the opposite. Now let's reverse the perspective to see how the donations from the industrial and financial sectors break down for both campaigns.

Table 5   Breakdown of Donations Made by Each Sector

	Donations made (in GBP and in percentage of the total donated by each sector)
Donations from industrial sectors (secondary and tertiary)	17,470,875.05
Leave campaign	44.5%
Remain campaign	55.5%
Donations from the financial sector	15,584,010.28
Leave campaign	65.5%
Remain campaign	34.5%

The breakdown of donations by financial and industrial sectors is even more telling. Almost two thirds of financial sector donations went to Leave groups, whereas under half of industrial sector donations were made in favour of the Leave campaign.

These puzzling figures raise many questions. Does this mean that the statements of City representatives in support of remaining within the European Union were mendacious? Did they publicly display support for the European Union and fund Brexit on the sly? On both counts, the answer is no. If we look at the detail of donations to the two campaigns, it appears that the financial sector was far from having a unanimous position on the referendum. Let us begin with a list of the financial subsectors involved in referendum donations.

Let's track the donations of financiers based on their subsector. A pattern appears, with two groups of financial subsectors emerging, one in favour of Leave and the other in favour of Remain.[15]

33

Table 6   Activity and Role of the Main Financial Subsectors

Financial subsector	Activity
Financial advice (audit, mergers and acquisitions [M&A], services)	These firms sell financial advice to the buyers and sellers of companies, and to the executives of these companies.
Financial communication (investors relations, market communication)	These firms help companies present their financial reports and communicate on their activity so as to be favourably evaluated by analysts.
Market information, brokerage services and foreign exchange services	These companies offer platforms for the sale and purchase of financial securities by individuals and professionals.
Banks (including investment banks)	Banks collect household savings and lend money to companies. Investment banks also help companies to access funding.
Institutional investors (including pension funds)	Institutional investors collect household savings through life insurance contracts or pension contracts. They invest these savings in compliance with regulations, acting on their own account or through other asset management companies.
Insurance	Insurers collect household savings via insurance contracts and invest them in compliance with regulations, acting on their own account or through other asset management companies.

Commodity trading	These companies speculate on the price of commodities on financial markets.
Hedge funds	These funds manage capital held by wealthy individuals, banks and institutional investors. They do not invest in companies, but rather in derivative products, such as securitised debt and options.
Private equity funds	These funds manage capital held by wealthy individuals, banks and institutional investors. They invest in companies that are not listed on the stock exchange.
Quantitative trading funds	These funds manage capital held by wealthy individuals, banks and institutional investors. They invest on financial markets using algorithmic instruments.
Real estate funds	These funds manage capital held by wealthy individuals, banks and institutional investors. They invest it in real estate properties.
Other alternative investment	These funds manage capital held by wealthy individuals and other sources. They invest in risky countries and sectors that are not covered by conventional asset managers.

Most of the financial subsectors show a tendency to support one or the other side of the referendum. Which leads us to a conclusion: while the financial sector as a whole seemed quite divided in its support, the choice of Leave or Remain was quite

Table 7   Campaign Funding by Financial Subsectors

Financial subsector	Recipient campaign	Amount donated (GBP)
Financial advice (including audit)	Remain	42,508.50
Financial communication	Remain	58,921.60
Banks (including investment banks)	Remain	767,000
Institutional investors (including pension funds)	Remain	889,756
Market information, brokerage	Remain	895,000
services and foreign exchange services	Leave	615,000
Insurance	Remain	55,000
	Leave	50,000
Real estate funds	Remain	45,000
	Leave	45,000
Commodity trading	Remain	150,000
Other alternative asset investment	Leave	2,106,374.76
Quantitative trading	Remain	1,210,000
Private equity funds	Remain	754,017
	Leave	1,944,296.27
Hedge funds	Remain	502,000
	Leave	5,447,136.15

consistent for all but two of the subsectors. Most financial subsectors donated to only one side. In the two main cases, private equity and hedge funds, where money was donated to both campaigns, the vast majority of the resources were directed to just one side. For instance, hedge fund managers made some donations to the Remain campaign, but 90 per cent of the money they gave went to the Leave side, as did over 70 per cent of the money given by private equity fund managers.

Overall, executives and companies in financial consulting, financial communication, financial information, brokering, foreign exchange, institutional investment (including pension funds), quantitative trading, banking (including investment banking) and insurance donated to the Remain campaign. Inversely, alternative asset managers, hedge funds and private equity funds invested heavily in the Leave campaign. What lies behind these diverging orientations? Do hedge funds, private equity funds and other alternative asset management companies share common characteristics that would explain their collective engagement in favour of the UK leaving the European Union? What, in short, are the economic interests that underly these distinct political and institutional choices?

To answer this question, we need to think in terms of modes of accumulation. Our hypothesis is that there are two ways in which capital circulates and accumulates in the financial sector, which we call 'first-wave' and 'second-wave' finance. These two types of financial activity make sense in a historical perspective, as we will discuss below. But before we enter into that discussion we want to describe the specific economic rationales of these two sets of actors (Table 8).

Table 8 First- and Second-Wave Finance Modes of Accumulation

	First-wave finance	*Second-wave finance*
Origin of capital	Public call for savings	Private solicitation of investors and financial intermediaries
Investment time frame	Liquid (short term)	Liquid (medium term)
Mode of funding in the economy	Equity through stock markets, debt	Equity outside of stock markets, securitised debt
Mode of asset management	Passive	Alternative
Mode of corporate control	Managerial (dissociation of property and control)	Shareholder-value-based (merging of property and control)
Preferred type of transaction	Public markets	Over-the-counter transactions

In first-wave finance accumulation of capital is characterised by public calls for savings that are collected by retail
savings institutions and invested for short periods of time
in shares acquired on listed markets. This mode of financial
accumulation does not involve financial players who take over
the companies in which they invest; they generally follow a
passive strategy and delegate the control of firms to managers.
Inversely, second-wave finance is characterised by players
who invest private capital (coming from wealthy individuals
and other professional investors) in unlisted assets; in the
medium term these players take active control of these assets.
This investment strategy is commonly referred to as 'alternative', in the sense that it is decorrelated from listed financial
markets, either because the investments are in unlisted firms
(such as the investments of private equity funds), or because
the funds are invested in derivatives, structured debt or other
complex financial products. The differences between first-
wave and second-wave financiers are not primarily differences
of individual background and careers, education, economic
beliefs, or differences in the technical and financial innova-
tions they use. What distinguishes the two groups is where
and how they invest, the kind of funding they raise and the
type of investment management they pursue – in other words,
they are not defined by social characteristics but by their mode
of accumulation.

Financial subsectors are not easily classed as first-wave or
second-wave finance, because the two modes of accumulation
often coexist within a single organisation. For instance, a bank
can invest money in a passive way on listed markets, which
would be characteristic of first-wave finance, while at the same
time running an in-house private equity fund that takes control
of firms in the wake of over-the-counter acquisitions, a typical
activity of second-wave finance. The distinction between
the two groups is necessarily subtle. Instead of decreeing a

hard and fast borderline, we understand these two modes of accumulation as ideal types, or polar cases, among which the various subsectors can be distributed. The first type of financial accumulation is embodied by banks, insurance companies and stock markets, whereas the second type is typified by hedge funds, private equity funds and, more broadly, asset managers who follow alternative investment strategies (Table 9).

Table 9 Activities of First- and Second-Wave Finance

First-wave finance	Second-wave finance
Financial advice (including audit)	Hedge funds
Financial communication	Private equity funds
Market information, brokerage services, foreign exchange services	Quantitative trading funds
Banks (including investment banks)	Real estate funds
Institutional investors (including pension funds)	Other alternative investors
Insurance	
Commodity trading	

Some activities fall between these two types of accumulation. This is the case for quantitative traders: the algorithmic instruments they use to make investment decisions are generally used on listed markets, but the traders' techniques are also massively used by hedge funds that collect money privately and speculate on complex financial products.

How did the representatives of these two modes of financial accumulation position themselves on the issue of Brexit? If we look at the campaign donations with this distinction between first- and second-wave finance in mind, then the situation becomes clear. The Remain side was funded primarily by first-wave financial entities, while the Leave side was massively supported by second-wave financial players.

Table 10   Proportion of Each Campaign's Funding Provided by
First- and Second-Wave Finance

	Donations/percentage of the total received by each campaign
Leave campaign	10,205,807.18
First-wave finance	6.5%
Second-wave finance	93.5%
Remain campaign	5,378,203.1
First-wave finance	53.3%
Second-wave finance	46.7%

The situation is particularly clear regarding the Leave campaign: 94 per cent of its financial support came from the ranks of second-wave finance. The Remain campaign is more evenly divided, with 53 per cent of donations coming from first-wave financial entities, and the remaining 47 per cent from firms and individuals belonging to second-wave finance. It should be noted, however, that a large proportion of this 47 per cent came from quantitative trading, which represents 22 per cent of financial sector donations to the Remain campaign. As we saw above, this subsector occupies a median position on the axis from the first to the second mode of financial accumulation. By their investment time frame, marketplace (listed markets) and investment strategy, quantitative traders look like first-wave financial actors. The origin of the funds they manage, and the fact that they are considered to be not passive but alternative asset managers, lead us to classify them as second-wave financial actors for the sake of analytic clarity. If we set aside their contribution to the overall amount, second-wave finance account for only 24 per cent of donations received by the Remain campaign, whereas first-wave finance accounts for 76 per cent.

On this basis we formulate the hypothesis that the mode of financial accumulation plays a determinant role in explaining how financial actors positioned themselves with respect to the Brexit referendum. This becomes even clearer when we look at how the money donated by each group of financial actors was distributed among the two campaigns (Table 11).

Table 11   Funding Choice of Each Financial Subsector During the Campaign

	Donations/percentage of the total donated to each campaign
First-wave finance	3,532,186.10
Leave campaign	18.8%
Remain campaign	81.2%
Second-wave finance	12,051,824.20
Leave campaign	79.2%
Remain campaign	20.8%

First-wave financial entities dedicated 81.2 per cent of their financial effort to keeping the UK within the EU, while second-wave entities channelled 79.2 per cent of their donations to the pro-Brexit side. These two distinct modes of capital appropriation, investment and accumulation thus appear to be strongly tied to distinct political objectives: the way in which financial actors accumulate money determines their support for the UK remaining in the EU or their preference for Brexit. According to good materialist logic, as Marx once said, 'it was therefore not so-called principles that kept these fractions [of the bourgeoisie] divided, but rather their material conditions of existence, two distinct sorts of property'.[16] The two modes of financial accumulation described here appear to be the source of divergent economic interests and hence opposing political orientations.

While first-wave financial entities are well known to the public, second-wave entities tend to remain in the shadows. First-wave finance led a public campaign with bold arguments pointing to the significance of the European financial passport and the importance of keeping clearing houses on UK soil. This campaign fielded well-established names and figures, including banks and insurance companies that have dominated the City for centuries, and whose very names are emblematic of what is commonly thought of as the financial sector. These entities operate in plain sight; the British stock markets are among the most powerful and the most scrutinised in the world, to the point that their quotations scroll in never-ending banners at the bottom of news screens. Inversely, second-wave financial actors keep remarkably quiet. Their companies are more recent, less well known, and, despite their profitability, they employ comparatively small numbers of people. The transactions in which they engage take place in the obscurity of over-the-counter exchanges and financial niches located at the margins of regulated activity. Most people could not name even one second-wave finance company. This is precisely why we need to understand who these second-wave financial entities are and what exactly it is they want.

Good financial reasons to leave the European Union – at last

More discreet than the Remain-backing financiers, those backing Leave also seem to have been more powerful, at least in terms of donations. Among them are billionaires and mul-timillionaires, whose fortunes are often recent and have been nurtured in the realm of alternative finance. This is the case for hedge fund managers, most of whom work in the West End, especially in the very posh Mayfair district. It is also the case for other figures in alternative asset management, and other polyvalent financiers specialised in operations carried out at the margins of the regulated financial markets. Some of them took positions publicly, including Crispin Odey, the founder of the hedge fund Odey Asset Management, whose wealth amounted to an estimated £900 million, and Michael Hintze, the founder of CQS, the fourth largest UK hedge fund, with a fortune worth some £1.6 billion. There was also Arron Banks, whose activities include exploiting diamond mines in South Africa and selling insurance policies to English motorists, but whose fortune of approximately £250 million derived mostly from a network of companies based in offshore jurisdictions such as Gibraltar and the Isle of Man and specialising in speculative niche insurance companies and 'wealth protection' services for high-net-worth individuals.[17]

Peter Hargreaves, whose wealth is estimated at £2.2 billion, was one of the most generous donors. He gave £3.2 million to Vote Leave Ltd. In 1981 he created Hargreaves Lansdown, an investment platform that made it possible for small investors to buy not only shares but also exchange-traded funds, stock trackers, derivatives and more complex financial products. The company now manages €73 billion in assets. Hargreaves stepped down from Hargreaves Lansdown in 2015. The following year, he launched the hedge fund Blue Whale Capital, in partnership with another hedge fund manager who came from Artemis Investment Management. He has also invested a growing portion of his personal wealth in Blue Whale Capital, with more than £250 million of it managed by the fund in 2022. Much of the rest of his fortune is managed by his family office – another financial investment structure with low regulatory requirements. David Buik is another Brexit supporter. This ardent promoter of the British financial sector is one of the most famous brokers in the country and frequently delivers his economic commentary on TV news networks. In June

2016 he asserted that an eventual Brexit would not impair the British financial sector. In his words: 'At the beginning, there will be troubles, of course. But we'll earn such a feeling of freedom. The City is strong enough to resist.'[18] What about JPMorgan Chase and HSBC, banks that threatened to partially relocate their headquarters to continental Europe in the event of Brexit? Buik said: 'I wish them very good holidays. Go to Europe if you want, but I'm telling you: you'll come back to London.' Paul Marshall, the founder of Marshall Wace, one of the biggest hedge funds in London, also expounded in 2017 to the *Financial Times*: 'Most people in Britain do not want to become part of a very large country called Europe. They want to be part of a country called Britain.' The financial support from this handful of financiers was decisive: the money paid by the top four donors (Crispin Odey, Arron Banks, Paul Marshall and Peter Hargreaves) amounted to 55 per cent of donations to Leave from the financial sector, and 30 per cent of all the donations received by the Leave side.

What spurred them to spend so much money? We will explore in greater depth the often murky ideological world of these actors in the following chapters. Here we will rapidly survey the views they expressed publicly in the press. Critical researchers have often emphasised that European regulation has resulted in the constitutionalisation of neoliberalism, a programme to confiscate the sovereignty of the people in the interest of capital, which as such has been a very good institutional deal for European capital markets.[19] It seems, however, that in the eyes of second-wave financial players Europe has not been accommodating enough. By leaving the European Union they hoped to gain a free hand to invest in the ways they wished and be rid of the financial regulations of Brussels, which they found too restrictive. To drive home their argument, they pointed to the mediocre economic performance of European Union countries, whose growth they claimed had been stifled by EU bureaucracy. The economist Savvas Savouri, of Toscafund Asset Management, said on 14 May 2016 that he was 'fed up with the anti-Brexit rhetoric' that was dominating the referendum campaign. 'All these economic threats sound fake to me', he continued. 'We have half a billion pounds invested in British real estate and companies. If we were worried about the economic consequences of the UK getting out of the European Union, we would say so. Quite the opposite, Brexit would represent a golden opportunity for the growth of the country.' In his view, the major risk to his financial sector was not leaving the European Union but remaining inside. Roger Bootle, founder of Capital Economics (a company that provides macroeconomic advice to financial actors) and a regular columnist for the *Daily Telegraph*, shared this analysis: 'By getting out of the European Union, we'll open up to the world. Look at the disastrous economic situation of Europe in the last two decades, compared to us, the United States and the rest of the world.'[20] Bootle's opinion was far from being marginal. He belonged to the Economists for Free Trade group (previously Economists for Brexit), made up of economists, not all academics, who habitually criticised the costs and constraints allegedly imposed by Brussels, and who considered Brexit an opportunity to launch a new cycle of financial deregulation in the UK. This discussion was clearly taking place within a broader controversy in which pro-Brexit groups were making the argument that European regulation was costly for the country as a whole. For instance, the Eurosceptic think tank Open Europe published a report in October 2013 asserting that the 100 EU regulations that were allegedly the most costly reduced the UK's gross domestic product by £27.4 billion a year.

Beyond this general anti-regulation position, pro-Brexit financiers also opposed the European Union on the narrower issue of financial regulations, accusing Brussels of trying to 'stifle the financial sector'. They described themselves as the collateral victims of the measures that punished the excessive risk-taking of bankers in the aftermath of the 2008 economic crisis. They were particularly angry that, from 2009, the European Union had enacted directives to regulate alternative investments. In February 2016, Paul Marshall wrote in the *Financial Times* that, 'rather than a rational, fact-based response, the [European] Commission launched an onslaught on hedge funds, leaving the banks and their lobbyists largely alone'. He then quoted a Belgium member of the European Parliament who, as he tells it, pointedly told him that 'if you are in a bar and a fight breaks out, you do not hit the person who started the fight but the person you have always wanted to hit'. From this viewpoint, the agreement signed on 18 February 2016 by David Cameron solved nothing. For second-wave financiers, it even sealed their failure to secure their main objective – a UK veto over European Commission decisions related to financial regulation.

Leaving the European Union also meant that they would have more opportunities to pursue deals and alliances with non-European countries without interference. Instead of a privileged but stifling relationship with EU countries, they preferred the ability to make deals with the rest of the world. Even though the UK was not part of the eurozone, they believed that belonging to the European Union reduced their monetary sovereignty. Brexit would in this respect be a way to decrease the value of the pound and attract foreign investors and clients. Martin Hughes, another economist and cofounder of Toscafund Asset Management, asserted that 'if the pound decreases, this will be good for the British GDP. Millions of wealthy Chinese and Indians will be attracted by real estate, luxury cars, and universities that will be cheaper for them.'

With their ambition of launching a new wave of financial deregulation, raising the prospect of attracting capital from all over the world, second-wave financial actors intended to turn the City into a kind of offshore centre for alternative investment. Former investment banker Marc Fiorentino explained that 'financiers are dreaming of turning London into a global Singapore, an area free of all European regulation, where all the emerging economic and financial forces could freely do their business, a vast land of asylum for tax evaders'.[21]

Contrary to what a superficial observation of the public positions taken by City bankers has led many to believe, an organised, powerful and determined group of financial actors in London supported their country leaving the European Union. The referendum was the story of the struggle between two modes of financial accumulation, two factions of the financial sector with antagonistic economic interests. To sustain its growth, the first group needed the European Union and its associated features – the European passport, the clearing mechanisms and the privilege of being the financial hub of the continent. The second group needed to break free of Brussels' oversight in order to reorganise the financial sector to suit the growing alternative finance sector.

Given the amount of money that a part of the financial sector spent on supporting Leave, it is a bit surprising to see how readily researchers and elites have accepted the interpretation of Brexit as a defeat of the establishment by the people. Echoing Joseph Stiglitz's analysis of the election of Trump as resulting from the 'discontents of globalisation', many have described the outcome of the Brexit vote as the expression of a rift between the winners and the losers of globalisation,[22] with the Remain side supported by wealthy and well-educated people living in big metropolitan areas, and the Leave side supported by voters from poor, neglected industrial wastelands and outlying regions. Even if the electoral geography of Brexit does show the significance of the popular vote in ensuring victory for the Leave side, the study of the electoral funding of Brexit reveals another phenomenon at work. Here, the winners of globalisation were not defeated by the losers. The Brexit referendum pitted winners against winners.

This finding belies critical thought that portrays those who benefit from the regulations of capitalist states as a homogeneous group, a unified social class with common economic interests and consequently common political goals. Works in this tradition of scholarship are often grounded on sociological analyses of the similarities in the social backgrounds, life stories and networks of members of the economic and political elite, but they tend to underestimate the diversity of interests found in the dominant classes.[23] According to this research, analysis of the individual characteristics of top civil servants and economic leaders supports an empirical description of the homogeneity of the dominant class.[24] Among those who accumulate capital, no conflict is possible: the elite are united by their shared experiences of schools, territories and lifestyles, forming a joint political programme. The concept of oligarchy used by Monique Pinçon-Charlot and Michel Pinçon summarises this analysis.[25] They use the term 'oligarchy' to characterise the social class that undertakes an organised appropriation of public goods for its own private benefit. The two sociologists write that

> there are considerable wealth inequalities within the bourgeoisie, and yet, despite this extreme dispersion, wealth is the basis of the existence of the bourgeoisie as a social class. [...] It exists *by itself* (*en-soi*) and *for itself* (*pour-soi*), and it can only exist if it combines these two ways of being. One can even wonder whether the bourgeoisie would be, in Western societies, the only social class worthy of the name.[26]

Here, there are no conflicts among accumulators, among the bourgeoisie. And the authors take another step; in their view, there is no conflict between accumulators and regulators. Public and private actors are seen to act harmoniously to strengthen the domination of the dominant class. This is also David Graeber's view, when he uses the concept of total bureaucracy to designate the 'progressive fusion of public and private authorities within a single entity, clogged with rules whose final objective is to extract wealth under the form of profit'.[27]

Despite their critical power, these analyses break with the materialist stance that defines the owners of capital not only by the exploitative relationship they maintain with workers but also by the competitive relationships that exist among themselves. When Marx described Bonapartism and the 1848 revolution, he told the story of the struggles between distinct factions of the bourgeoisie, whose modes of accumulation and political programmes diverged. These oppositions, he analysed, fundamentally explained the movement of history. This is also the sense of the recent critique addressed by the economic sociologist Jens Beckert to his colleague Kurtulus Gemici:

> The organization of the economy is not just about making complex social interactions possible but about 'who gets what' [...] Coordination in the economy is not just about establishing an order but is also a struggle for social structures – institutions, networks, cognitive scripts – that shape the economic field in ways advantageous to the actors advocating the structure.[28]

By the time the result of the referendum became known on 24 June 2016, financiers from both sides had been competing for months to obtain an institutional arrangement favourable to their interests. For backers of Leave and Remain alike the political event of Brexit reconfigured their opportunities and interests. For first-wave financial actors, the new situation obliged them to find ways to safeguard their holdings and not lose everything: they had to reinvent their institutional modalities of accumulation in a degraded context. For second-wave financiers, the goal was simpler: to press home their advantage and consolidate their newly acquired hegemony.

2

Second-Wave Finance vs the European Union

The insurgency of parts of the financial sector seems incongruous given the extent to which the construction of the European Union fostered the resurrection of London as a global financial hub once the United Kingdom entered the European Economic Community (EEC) in 1973. Indeed, the European construction and the Anglo-American financialisation of Europe advanced side by side at first. However, they diverged in the wake of the 2008 financial crisis. At that time European institutions were pressured by continental governments to regulate the excesses of the new financial sectors that had emerged in the 2000s, and the EU acted quickly to rein them in.

The United Kingdom, dissatisfied sovereign of Europe's financialisation

To understand how it was in the interest of the City to support the development of European institutions we must go back to 1973. At the time there were two financial sectors in the City of London, not just one. The traditional financial sector was still in place, the City that existed before the first wave of financialisation in the 1970s and 1980s. It was made up of large banking conglomerates (some of which were state-owned), family-owned brokerage companies, insurers specialised in international trade, and commodity traders. Historically this traditional City owed its existence to corporatist regulation of the sector – for instance, the fact that one needed to acquire a broker's licence to access the stock exchange – and it remained modest in size. But this traditional sector was declining. In the 1960s and 1970s there emerged a new set of financiers in the City, which we call first-wave financial actors. They included in their ranks 'foreign banks settled in London (most of them from the US and Japan), overseas banks and British investment banks (or merchant banks)'.[1] These entities attracted international capital and financed large European companies. They brought to the UK the practices of US investment banks, importing the financialisation movement initiated in the United States as early as the 1960s.

These two Cities saw the construction of Europe quite differently. For the traditional City, European integration raised deeply worrying prospects. Since the end of the Second World War the power of the City had been waning compared to that of New York. The London banks lost their historical supremacy to their American competitors in the 1950s, in terms of monetary amounts managed. The primacy of London over other European centres was also weakening. From 1962 to the big bang of the 1980s, London ceded its top place to Zurich in terms of amounts of initial public offerings and bond issuances. The London Stock Exchange had become a stock exchange dedicated to national companies.[2] This had negative consequences for the family-owned stockbrokers that operated on London exchanges, as they had fewer transactions to handle. In short, the traditional City was in a very poor position to confront international and European competition.

Inversely, first-wave financial entities benefited from this competition. Foreign investment banks that had recently set up in London profited from the boom of the eurodollars market, which dealt in bonds and other forms of credit denominated in dollars and dedicated to European companies. Despite the lobbying of the traditional City, these entities were favoured by very lenient regulation and the UK became the gateway for US capital entering the European continent. In 1973, 80 per cent of dollar-denominated funds raised in Europe were concentrated in London. These flows were handled by investment banks that are representative of first-wave finance actors.

In the 1960s and 1970s, these actors actively pushed the United Kingdom to join the EEC. Siegmund Warburg was a typical player of first-wave finance. He had founded in the 1950s an investment bank (Warburg) on the US model. He was the main architect of the eurodollars market and became 'one of the most powerful City bankers' in the 1970s.[3] He was close to both Labour and Conservative policymakers, a personal friend of the prime minister Harold Wilson, and he advocated for the UK to join the EEC. As early as 1971, he promoted 'the strengthening of co-operation between Britain and North America and between Britain and the European Continent' so as to create the 'transatlantic triangle' that was optimal for his business.[4] Warburg was a striking example of the dependency of these new financial practices on British and then European regulation. The exchange of eurodollars relied on a set of national regulations, laws and later European directives that allowed the Warburg bank to organise the circulation of dollar flows in Europe. These rules and institutional actions were necessary conditions for the Warburg bank to turn a profit, and for the personal enrichment of its owner. They formed what we call an 'institutional arrangement' that underpinned the circulation of capital and the extraction of profit. Such institutional arrangements are constructed, developed and maintained by the political regime in which they are embedded. The institutional architecture that first-wave finance obtained in the 1980s was not born ex nihilo. It was the fruit of the election of Margaret Thatcher in 1979, of the

British electoral and party system that brought Thatcher to power, and of the new international order that was being put in place at the same time by the United States under Ronald Reagan. Recognition of the fact that the financial sector needs the power of institutions to grow and accumulate capital is not new. In the 1940s, Karl Polanyi described how in the late nineteenth century *haute finance* was dependent on the 'concert of nations', itself organised along lines established by a set of parties, political customs, constitutional rules and geopolitical relationships.[5] To distinguish between the institutional arrangement of legal rules that allows capital to circulate and the political regime that spawns this arrangement, we call the latter a 'political regime of accumulation'. Tracking dominant economic interests in the UK, we identify two political regimes of accumulation from the end of the Second World War to the 1990s (Table 12).

The traditional City perceived the European construction as a political instrument designed to allow first-wave financial entities to replace the traditional financial establishments. Integration into the EEC opened the UK to European capital and put an end to the Fordist accumulation regime that had prevailed until then. The business community 'saw in the Common Market [...] an instrument to demolish *dirigiste* national structures'.[6] The Thatcher government used integration in the Common Market as a reason to abruptly abolish the Treasury's control on capital flows in 1979. Outflows of British capital rose rapidly: the percentage of assets held by British investors in foreign institutions doubled in 1980.[7] This flow of capital escaped the monopoly of the traditional City, to the benefit of first-wave financiers. The Common Market became a key element in the political regime of accumulation that fostered the development of first-wave financial entities.

With the support of emerging international firms in the City, the Thatcher government imposed so-called deregulation

Table 12   Financial Sectors and Political Regimes of Accumulation in the United Kingdom from the 1950s to the 1990s

Financial sectors	Traditional City	First-wave finance
Period of domination	Up to the 1970s	From the 1970s to the 1990s
Emblematic entities	Retail banks, international trade services, family-owned brokerage companies	Investment banks, institutional investors, pension funds
Mode of asset management	Active (investing in a limited number of companies thought to be lucrative)	Passive (distributing the risk among all available investments on the market)
Mode of corporate control	Public (oversight by public authorities)	Managerial (control exercised by executives of the firm)
Type of intermediation	Financial system dominated by banks	Financial system dominated by the stock market
Institutional arrangement of the financial sector	Financial sector under direct state control	Regulated financial sector
Type of economy	State-controlled credit-based economy	Financial market economy
International institutions	Monetary system organised under the Bretton Woods agreement. World demand is supported by a network of institutional organisations (IMF, World Bank).	Flexible exchange system. International institutions are weakened by new organisations, such as the G7 and the European Union. Economic policies are influenced by the consensus in Washington D.C.
Political regime of accumulation	Fordist regime based on a redistributive welfare state	Financialised regime based on a regulating state and a social safety net
Ideological framework	Keynesianism	The Austrian and Chicago schools

55

measures on the London Stock Exchange, triggering what became known as the 1986 'big bang'. The corporatist rules that had limited access to the stock exchange were abolished, and overnight international banks and brokers were allowed to handle trades there. The Securities and Investment Board (SIB) was made responsible for regulating trades, replacing regulation by the Treasury and industry ministerial departments. The board was composed of both civil servants and members from the financial sector. This big bang was part of a wider deregulation movement. Between 1979 and 1989, the successive Thatcher governments had Parliament enact ten laws related to financial deregulation. These laws removed the regulations that limited issuance of credit by banks (June 1980), and then eliminated the liquidity ratios imposed on banks up to this point (August 1981). Consumer loans were deregulated (July 1982), and issuance of housing mortgages was spurred by allowing non-mutual corporations and especially stock listed companies to grant housing loans (1986).

These changes were disastrous for traditional City actors. For a family of brokers such as that of the Eurosceptic leader Nigel Farage – the son of a broker, the brother of a broker, and a broker himself at the London Metals Exchange – they brought not only the loss of 'the best gentleman's club in the world', but also considerable personal financial setbacks.[8] Despite the speculative bubbles and the stock exchange crashes that occurred from 1987 onwards, the big bang of 1986 was a success for the emerging first-wave financiers. Within a few years London was again able to compete with Wall Street.

But the Common Market served a wider purpose than just the City's palace revolutions. The United Kingdom was also developing a plan for Europe, in the form of a financialised common market ruled by the London-based financial sector. The coalition of emerging British financiers and large foreign banks that had forged the 'financial roots of European integration' was particularly active in the 1980s.[9] Assuming the role of spokesperson for the newly dominant factions of its financial sector, the British government took the lead in EEC economic policy. This was especially clear starting with the first Delors Commission. Jacques Delors was the candidate favoured by Margaret Thatcher for president of the European Commission. He came with all the guarantees of a good neoliberal temperament that first-wave finance was looking for. Surrounded by technocrats, he had deregulated the French banking and financial sector a few years earlier, and had formed a European Commission dominated by free-marketeers. The Single European Act of 1986 was elaborated under the supervision of the British commissioner to the Common Market chosen by Thatcher herself, Arthur Cockfield, who had already been in charge of abolishing controls on capital and negotiating the financial big bang with the London Stock Exchange in his own country. From 1985 to 1995, the successive Delors commissions demolished the last interventionist institutions remaining from the postwar period and left the field free for the emerging financial entities.

The Single European Act presented the freedom of circulation as a constitutive principle of the 'territory without inner borders' that was expected to be in place by 1992. But the notion of free circulation was understood in economic terms: circulation of goods, circulation of capital, free trade of services. In 1999, the Financial Services Action Plan (FSAP) pursued the integration of European capital markets. It led to the Lamfalussy process and the Markets in Financial Instruments Directive (MIFID). The plan called for abolition of brokerage monopolies in the countries where they still existed, as in France, leading to integration of the French stock exchange into Euronext. The FSAP also instituted financial 'passporting', which allowed companies registered in one

European country to distribute financial products throughout the European Union. This broad process then led to action plans with benefits for each financial subsector. For instance, private equity funds benefited from their own action plan, the Venture Capital Action Plan (VCAP) for the funding of non-listed companies. This was designed to stimulate the growth of this emerging sector and increase its profitability. To promote the development of certain sectors, European authorities also left some activities in the regulatory shadows. One example was over-the-counter financial derivatives, which remained unregulated.

With the European Union now the keystone of a political regime of accumulation favourable to London's first-wave finance, this could have been the end of the story. But in the late 1990s, first-wave finance began to run out of steam. Financial operators had recovered from what David Harvey called the 'capitalist crisis of accumulation' of the 1970s.[10] But although financiers had thrived and accumulated capital for two decades, the pace of their accumulation was slowing. At the same time, new financial sectors were emerging in the United States, sectors that operated outside of conventional stock markets and were starting to threaten the position of London-based first-wave finance. Offshore financial centres were beginning to compete with London financial entities and divert a significant share of capital from their business. First-wave financiers in the UK were unnerved. As they pondered how to revive their business a new threat emerged: a nebula of new financial sectors that were still low-profile, but rapidly developing into a second wave of new financial practice. These new financial companies were based on aggressive business models and for the most part unregulated. They raised funds from first-wave financial institutions and then ploughed them into medium-term investments via over-the-counter transactions (real estate, non-listed companies, derivatives, high-risk structured loans), a hidden continent that had been left unexplored by first-wave finance. For instance, large British banks launched the first UK private equity funds, dedicated to investing in non-listed companies: HSBC launched Charterhouse Capital Partners in 1982, and NatWest launched NatWest Equity Partners in 1984. These new activities flourished so well that they grew their own wings and took off to fly on their own. NatWest Equity Partners split off from NatWest to become Bridgepoint Advisers in 2000, and Charterhouse became independent of HSBC in 2001. These entities came to form a distinct group, second-wave finance, with its own set of interests.

Such activities emerged in the gaps of the political regime of accumulation favourable to first-wave finance. The European Union had long ago made the choice to delegate financial regulation to financial actors, promoting a 'lax regulation' ensured by bodies with no real power. In the words of Margot Sève:

> green books, white books, action plans, statements, conclusions, recommendations, resolutions, codes of conduct: such instruments are alternative instruments to legislation, they have a para-legal function, as they aim to operate political choices, including regulatory choices, for all the member states without having to follow the cumbersome legislative procedure required by the European treaties.[11]

Over the years this lax approach created a number of shadowy areas in European financial regulation. The second wave of financial entities that appeared in the 1980s and 1990s benefited from this, as can be seen in the following table comparing the economic, institutional and political dimensions of the political regimes of accumulation that characterise first- and second-wave finance (Table 13).

Table 1.3   Financial Sectors and Political Regimes of Accumulation in the United Kingdom from the 1990s to Today

Financial sectors	First-wave finance	Second-wave finance
Period of domination	From the 1970s to the 1990s	From the 2000s to today
Emblematic actors	Investment banks, institutional investors, pension funds	Hedge funds, private equity funds, real estate funds
Mode of asset management	Passive (distributing the risk among all the available investment on the market)	Alternative (investing outside of stock markets or in high-risk sectors and countries)
Mode of corporate control	Managerial (the control is ensured by the executives of the firm)	Shareholder-value (the control is ensured by the shareholders of the firm)
Type of intermediation	Financial system dominated by the stock market	Financial system dominated by actors operating outside of the stock market
Institutional arrangement of the financial sector	Regulated financial sector	Financial sector relying on mechanisms to avoid regulations
Type of economy	Financial market economy	Economy based on over-the-counter financial transactions
International institutions	Flexible exchange system. International institutions are weakened by new organisations, such as the G7 and the European Union. Economic policies are influenced by the consensus in Washington D.C.	Free circulation of capital. Competition between financial centres, promoted by the generalisation of IFRS norms and the Lamfalussy process. Transfer of financial and monetary regulation competency from the IMF to the Financial Stability Forum.

Political regime of accumulation	Financialised regime based on a regulating state and a social safety net	Financialised regime based on an authoritarian state with restricted social and civil rights
Ideological project	The Austrian and Chicago schools	Libertarianism (an extension of some aspects of the Austrian school)

It should be noted here that the distinction we make between first- and second-wave finance is not entirely congruent with other recent conceptual distinctions. In the last few years, political economists and sociologists have constructed new concepts to grasp the diverging interests of the financial sector. Particularly interesting are the patrimonialism concept developed by Megan Tobias Neely, and the asset management capitalism concept developed by Benjamin Braun. Neely argues that a key distinction within the financial sector today is between patrimonial financial actors, which are owned by their top managers (commonly through the legal form of partnerships), and non-patrimonial ones, which are owned by other shareholders (for instance, through the stock exchange).[12] Our categorisation is quite consistent with Neely's distinction, given that the vast majority of second-wave finance actors (including private equity, real estate and hedge funds) are organised as partnerships, i.e. they belong to their partners, and fit the patrimonialism concept. It seems to us, however, that this characteristic is not the single driving force behind their economic model and political position. Benjamin Braun's asset management capitalism is another interesting description of new oppositions in the financial sector:[13] the rise of asset managers, including both general asset managers such as BlackRock and Pimco and specialised alternative asset managers such as hedge funds and private equity funds, is indeed a key characteristic of today's capitalism. However, looking at political donations, we do not see a consistent political front formed by asset managers in the case of Brexit. Asset managers as defined by Braun are divided between alternative asset managers (e.g. private equity funds), which we class in the second-wave finance category, and mainstream asset managers, which we class in first-wave finance. Companies such as BlackRock, for instance, perform asset management in a more passive way than alternative investors do, preferring buying small stakes in large numbers of listed corporations than taking majority stakes as private equity funds do, but they also invest in private equity or real investment funds (through funds of funds), a practice that is emblematic of alternative management. In other words, we believe it is the mode of investment, rather than the legal form, that determines the political interest of financial actors and their economic underpinnings.

Going back to the rise of second-wave finance, the 2000s were years of extraordinary growth for these kinds of companies. During this period of intense accumulation, they acquired their independence and spawned billionaires who, thanks to their fortunes, would be able to massively fund referendums and elections a decade later. London became the hegemonic financial centre in Europe for all the activities emblematic of second-wave finance, and harboured its growth for two decades. These operators had a near-monopoly on European alternative asset management: with $400 billion under management, second-wave finance garnered 80 per cent of European hedge fund assets (and 20 per cent of global hedge fund assets). It also had a hegemonic hold on derivative trading. In 2007, 47 per cent of global international derivatives trading was done in London. London also dominated over-the-counter derivative trading in 2007, with 43 per cent of the market for these products in Europe.[14]

But this impressive growth suddenly came to a halt in 2008. Second-wave financial activities had enjoyed the safety of anonymity until then, but the financial crisis put them in the crosshairs of political and media attention. European policy-makers on the continent pounced on the idea that the solution to the crisis was 'to curb the City and the deregulated Anglo-American finance'.[15] Beyond responsibility for the financial crisis that was attributed to the exuberant development of second-wave finance, the desire to reign in these activities also resulted from power relationships in Europe. Second-wave finance was a recent phenomenon, and its component sectors did not have the same influence on continental political powers as did their first-wave finance peers. In most European countries other than the United Kingdom, second-wave financial sectors were still minority sectors. In Germany for instance, the hedge fund sector was almost nonexistent in 2008, France and Italy had some private equity and real estate funds, but their second-wave financial sectors were hardly comparable in size to British activity. The UK was at the forefront of European financialisation, and second-wave finance was on the verge of becoming a hegemonic force there. Not only was continental Europe less financialised than the UK, but within its financial sector second-wave financial actors were largely dominated by first-wave entities. In other words, the dominant class in the UK was a dominated class in the European Union.

As a consequence, the postcrisis period was very unfavourable to British second-wave finance. First-wave financial sectors, other member states and European authorities themselves were eager to put blame for the 2008 crisis on the emerging and unregulated financial sectors that were characteristic of second-wave finance. Regulations were quickly put into place to limit their power of accumulation. One such regulation was the Alternative Investment in Financial Markets (AIFM) directive of 2011 that imposed new controls by national regulators over alternative investors, that is to say over second-wave finance. This directive provoked a struggle, and between 2009 and 2011 the member states positioned themselves according to the strength of their respective second-wave financial sectors. Germany, France and Italy supported the directive, while the United Kingdom did all it could to water it down, with the help of Ireland and Luxembourg.[16] These efforts failed. David Cameron voted against the directive at the European Council of 14 May 2010, but it was finally adopted on 8 June 2011.

More broadly, the very principle of lax regulation was questioned. The financial sectors that had grown up in the gaps in regulations and prospered throughout the 1990s and 2000s were suddenly subject to regulation as of 2010. The ability of banks to make loans unscrutinised by European banking regulations was affected. The Capital Requirement Directives (CRD 3 and CRD 4) of 2010 and 2013 limited securitisation and shadowy banking practices by integrating them into the calculation of financial institutions' capital requirements. To reduce excessive individual risk-taking, the 2013 directive also limited the size of bonuses awarded to bankers and asset managers, to the great displeasure of British investment banks. The European Market Infrastructure Regulation (EMIR) of 2012 regulated over-the-counter trading in derivatives, an activity pursued by many hedge funds.

The European structure that had sheltered second-wave finance was suddenly less attractive. The UK's Investment Association, which represents British institutional investors, trounced the AIFM directive as 'perverse' and demanded that it not be applied in the country. The professional associations of the second-wave sector ceaselessly opposed the directive at all stages of legislative procedure. The British lobby for private equity funds, the British Venture Capital Association (BVCA), called the directive 'costly' and 'damaging' to the sector, while the hedge funds represented by the Alternative Investment Management Association declared that it 'would represent a serious and, in European financial services legislation, unprecedented attempt at closing Europe's borders'.[17] This directive stood so firmly in the way of their interests that some hedge fund managers threatened to flee the European Union and relocate to Switzerland. Although the 2015 negotiations on the single capital market allowed Cameron's government to try – unsuccessfully – to secure regulations more amenable to British financiers, the break between European public authorities and second-wave financial actors was consummated.

Faced with a neoliberal political regime of accumulation that no longer protected the institutional arrangement they thought was needed to ensure them increasing profits, second-wave financial actors found a potential way out: a change of political regime. If the British government, constrained by European law to which it was bound by supranational ties, was itself unable to change the political regime, the political regime would have to be discarded. Second-wave financial operators wanted to be rid of neoliberal institutions and invent something else. The good news for them was that in the mid-2010s they now had the resources to back their ambitions. After two decades of considerable profit accumulation, they were able to weigh in on politics through the fortunes that their companies and bosses had amassed. This did not bode well for UK membership in the European Union.

Newfound independence for finance in Europe after Brexit

As Brexit unfolded, financial sectors in other European countries began to reorganise in various ways according to the power relationships existing between first- and second-wave financial actors in these countries. Overall, first-wave financiers hoped to take advantage of the weakening of British financial institutions to capture a share of their profits. As for second-wave operators, they intended to take advantage of the victory of British second-wave finance to advance their agenda of breaking with neoliberalism and opening a new wave of deregulation in their own countries.

By undermining the role of the City as a gateway between Europe and the rest of the world for the flow of capital, Brexit weakened some first-wave financial actors. European financial markets tumbled after the announcement of the referendum result and the unforeseen turmoil in financial circuits. The valuation of many companies crumbled, especially in southern European countries: the main Milan stock exchange index lost 12.5 per cent on 24 June 2016, its Madrid equivalent lost 12.2 per cent, and its Athens equivalent 13.4 per cent.

The banking sector, a core component of first-wave finance, also suffered from the shock. Large Italian banks such as UniCredit, Intesa Sanpaolo, BPM and Banco Popolare, the largest Spanish bank Santander, and the French banks Société Générale and BNP Paribas, all lost more than 20 per cent of their valuation on 24 June 2016. Up through 2015 many continental banks had opened branches in London to gain access to the £3,400 billion of European and international assets that were available in the largest European financial centre.[18] In 2016 BNP Paribas employed 6,600 people in London. A few weeks before the referendum, the German banking regulator BaFin noted that 'Brexit would deal a strong blow to the largest German banks', since they conducted 'a large part of their activity in London, and with London'.

Brexit also affected the insurance sector. The valuation of the insurance giants fell: the French company Axa lost 15.1 per cent, the German Allianz 9.8 per cent and the French reinsurer Scor 7.8 per cent. At the time, any continental insurance company registered in its country of origin was authorised to sell insurance services to customers in the UK. In 2016 some 739 insurers and 5,700 intermediaries from the continent benefited from this access to the British market. For the banking sector, the economic shock for continental insurers was not primarily that they might lose their authorisation to sell insurance contracts directly to British customers (the UK was only the seventh largest market for Axa, representing no more than 5 per cent of its sales); the major threat stemmed from the role of the London market in capital investment. The capital collected by insurance companies (including life insurance) was broadly invested in London. Brexit forced the London branches of continental banks to relocate, and it also triggered relocation of their capital assets. By September 2019, no less than €75 billion worth of insurance assets had been shifted from London to continental Europe.

The victory of British second-wave financial actors was not a disappointment for all financial operators on the continent, however. Brexit was perceived by second-wave financial actors as an opportunity to compete with British firms and to increase the pressure on first-wave financial actors in their respective countries. Continental investment funds very quickly found reasons to rejoice over the result of the referendum. Even though Luxembourg and Dublin were already powerful in traditional asset management, Brexit was expected to push some alternative investment funds to open branches on the continent. The CEO of the investment fund Fuchs Asset Management declared to *Hedgeweek* in 2017 that 'Brexit is a huge opportunity for Luxembourg because new companies will be established, or for those who already have their own companies here, they will likely need to increase their substance and employ more people.'

Brexit was also a windfall for continental private equity funds. The chairman of Invest Europe, a lobbying group for these funds in Europe, noted that Brexit was going to 'make it harder to raise funds ... for the main private equity funds in London, whose capital comes mostly from continental

Europe', and that this would benefit continental funds. The French lobby for private equity funds, Afic, revelled over Brexit in 2017. Its chairman Olivier Millet stated that 'French private equity will overtake British assets by 2020.'

We must not let our understanding of the positions of continental member states of the EU on Brexit be distorted by assumptions about the Anglophilia (or phobia) of their people, or their respect (or disrespect) for democratic referendums. Rather these were national positions influenced by the weight of the financial sector in national economies, by the relative strength of their various components, and by their respective places in the European financial order, which until then had been dominated by London. Table 14 reviews the weight of the financial sector in the economies of the United Kingdom, the United States and the European Union and the weight of financial subsectors.

Table 14   Economic Weight of the Financial Sector and Second-Wave Finance in Western Countries in 2018[19]

	Share of the financial sector in GDP	Number of jobs in the financial sector	Share of the assets managed by second-wave finance
United Kingdom	7.0%	1,100,000	12.4%
United States	7.7%	6,300,000	11.8%
European Union (including the UK)	4.6%	3,800,000	6.4%

The seemingly modest size of the financial sector in European economies should not obscure its extraordinary profit-making capacities. In 2018, when the financial sector amounted to no more than 7 per cent of British GDP, financial corporations represented 22.7 per cent of the profits of listed companies. And when British listed companies made £64,735 of profit per employee on average, the major private equity fund 3i took in an exceptional profit of £5.2 million per employee. The financial sector thus generated far more profit than other sectors compared to its GDP share. It also fuelled far greater enrichment of its founders and executives than other sectors.

Table 15   Economic Weight of the Financial Sector and Second-Wave Finance in Europe in 2018[20]

	Share of the financial sector in GDP	Number of jobs in the financial sector	Share of assets managed by second-wave finance
United Kingdom	7.0%	1,100,000	12.4%
France	4.1%	859,000	5.3%
Germany	3.8%	1,300,000	N/A (very low: almost nonexistent)
Ireland	7.2%	101,300	13.1%

Continental governments reacted to Brexit according to the structure of their business community and the economic (and, consequently political) weight of second-wave financial actors within their financial sector. In Germany, the position of the government on Brexit reflected first and foremost the interests of German industrial exporters. Before Brexit, German companies posted an exceptionally large commercial surplus with the United Kingdom: €48.5 billion in 2015. In addition, the German financial sector, and especially its first-wave financial subsectors, relied heavily on London for their operations. In 2018 no less than 42 per cent of the assets of the leading German bank Deutsche Bank, some €600 billion, were managed in London. These actors sought to maintain the links between the City and the Single Market. Under their pressure the German finance ministry even studied internally the possibility of an 'integrated financial market' between Germany and the UK after Brexit.[21] It comes as no surprise that the German government adopted a conciliatory tone with the British during the Brexit negotiations. Regarding financial regulations, it merely repatriated German banks and the financing of German companies to Germany. Inversely, the lobby for German investment funds, speaking for the (modest) interests of second-wave finance in the country, wrote in 2017 that 'most asset managers based in London already have a branch in Luxembourg and/or in Dublin and have consequently already set foot in the European Union: we forecast far fewer relocations [to Germany] than in the banking sector'.[22] In other words, Germany was so far behind in the race to attract second-wave financial activities that their German representatives did not see Brexit as a significant opportunity.

The French government took a more aggressive position than Germany in the Brexit negotiations. The situation of France was paradoxical. Second-wave financial actors had a significant role in the economy, but the neoliberal option remained politically dominant. In addition, Paris was a well-positioned financial hub and its actors hoped that Brexit would reduce the influence of the City in Europe and that some of its business would come to Paris. French financiers unanimously supported the toughest possible position with respect to Brexit. The French alternative investment sector openly campaigned to provoke a 'hard' Brexit. As the vice-president of the asset management lobby Association France Gestion (AFG) put it, 'asset management is very easy to outsource, and France is well-positioned in Europe in the post-Brexit world'. The French regulatory bodies for financial markets and banks, the Autorité des Marchés Financiers (AMF) and the Autorité de Contrôle Prudentiel et de Résolution (ACPR), pushed for the relocation of British asset management companies to France through the creation of fast-track procedures for regulatory approval, which they called a '2 Week Ticket'. Under this accelerated process a British company could know whether it was certified by French authorities or not in under two weeks. Paris also intended to benefit from the relocation of clearing houses. In this sector the London branch of LCH was in competition with its Paris branch and with the German clearing house Eurex. The French government decided to back the Paris-based clearing house against both British and German interests, and sided with LCH to lobby European regulators to persuade them to concentrate all euro-denominated clearing operations in a single clearing house, the Paris branch of LCH. In France even first-wave financial actors ultimately welcomed Brexit as good news. The day after the vote, and despite the slipping valuation of his company, Frédéric Oudéa, CEO of the Société Générale bank and chairman of the French Banking Federation (FFB), asserted that 'the United Kingdom, out of the European Union, should also be taken out of the single European market and should be considered as a third-party country'. Brexit also made France the biggest market in the European Union for the insurance sector, which represented a 'unique opportunity for Paris' according to the newspaper of the French insurance sector *L'Argus de l'assurance*.

Beyond this diversity of approaches, national financial sectors encouraged their governments to influence the Brexit negotiations in their favour. National administrations became the sales representatives of their local financial centres. In France, both right-wing and left-wing policymakers coalesced in a 'holy union' to attract British financial companies to Paris. Valérie Pécresse, the president of the Île-de-France region, which includes Paris, borrowed a slogan from David Cameron and proposed to 'roll out the blue-white-red carpet' to financial companies willing to relocate to Paris. The region also placed advertisements in the *Financial Times* the week after the vote, wittily entitled 'Welcome to the Paris region'. Not surprisingly, the French president François Hollande (Socialist Party) also reiterated the demands of the financial sector lobby Paris Europlace when he said on 29 June 2016 that 'the United Kingdom enjoyed derogations for a long time, whereas it was not part of the eurozone. This will not be possible anymore. [...] The City, thanks to the European Union, was able to handle clearing operations of euro-denominated transactions although it was not in the eurozone – it will lose this ability.'

Brexit also revived the race between member states to attract financial activities, which the absolute supremacy of London had rendered vain. At the end of 2016, financial sector lobbies engaged in ambivalent communication, issuing both aggressive publicity designed to attract financial companies still located in London, and plaintive interviews encouraging their local governments to take stronger fiscal and regulatory measures against London. Even though the Euronext Bruxelles company hoped to benefit from Brexit, its chairman declared in the name of the Brussels-based financial sector that 'we have some strengths: no tax on capital or capital gains is an advantage. But the taxation on labour is still fairly high, even if it is moving in the right direction.' Regarding the tax on financial transactions that was being debated in the European Union at the time, he aimed his criticism directly at the Belgian government: 'We are not mature enough in Belgium to understand what financial markets really bring to us.' Brexit allowed European governments to justify their turnaround on this tax. In France, for instance, a tax on financial transactions was included in candidate François Hollande's presidential campaign programme in 2012, and written into the budget bill for 2017. But under president Emmanuel Macron, the prime minister Edouard Philippe, speaking at a lobbying meeting entitled 'Turning Paris into the foremost financial centre of post-Brexit Europe', announced that the tax measure would be dropped, stating that it 'was inapplicable and ... strongly penalised Paris as a financial centre'. A few months later the project was abandoned at the European level as well.

Continental financial sectors also opened new fronts in the fiscal competition between states. In France, Gérard Mestrallet, then president of the lobbying group Paris Europlace, declared that policymakers had to 'improve the competitiveness of Paris as a financial centre' following Brexit, and offered five proposals: eliminate the highest tax bracket for earned income; reduce taxes on capital and dividends; increase fiscal incentives for holding securities; simplify taxation on capital gains; drop the tax on financial transactions. The French government heeded his recommendations. The French Parliament voted to cap at 30 per cent the tax rate paid by hedge fund managers on their bonuses. Similar movements occurred in many other member states, and in European regions. The German Land of Hessen, where Frankfurt-am-Main is located, revised its labour law applicable to very highly paid employees to make it converge with British legislation. In Italy the government cut taxes for the highest income brackets and created a special regime for expatriates returning from London.

Brexit triggered a vast reconfiguration of European capital circuits, but this did not weaken the European financial sector. On the contrary, Brexit provoked a strengthening of its claims and rights to accumulate profits. The competition between national financial centres played out as a contest between national legislations. Weighing the merits and drawbacks of the legislation of each country, as in a double-entry ledger, continental financial sectors used Brexit to overcome the last remaining obstacles to financial accumulation. Not all segments of the financial sector have benefited from this reconfiguration in the same proportion, however. The race to produce the most attractive legislation directly benefited second-wave finance, but first-wave financial actors had to deal with a more uncertain situation, as Brexit called into question the ideal organisation of capital circuits that they had built up over decades. They also had to deal with an unfavourable geopolitical context: one of the flagship institutions of the political regime of accumulation that had supported their development was now weakened, and new financial firms were competing with them even in continental Europe. For first-wave finance, the (profitable) competition between member states to attract London bank branches to the continent came on top of a conflict with other segments of the financial sector that it was not certain to win.

Negotiating the exit from the European Union

Winning a referendum is not always enough to win the political game. The history of the construction of Europe shows how easily the outcome of referendums can be subverted. After the Brexit vote many steps had to be taken before second-wave finance could build the political regime of accumulation that it wanted, and there were numerous obstacles to overcome. Institutions are not easily killed off. The neoliberal institutions of the previous political regime of accumulation, which had been built up since the 1970s, were still supported by powerful players and resisted overhaul. Lobbyists from the industrial and first-wave financial sectors, rebellious ministers, pro-Remain MPs, the Speaker of the House of Commons, Conservative and Labour Party staff, technocrats, judges, the British Supreme Court – after the referendum victory the institutional landscape was full of actors who could and would oppose the political aims of second-wave finance.

The history of the post-referendum negotiations (see chronology in Table 16) is the record of the steps by which pro-Brexit financial actors converted their economic and financial power into a real political and institutional hegemony. We describe this series of successive conflicts below.

Table 16 Chronology of the Crisis of the Neoliberal Political Regime in the United Kingdom and the Reconfiguration of British Institutions

Date	Event
23 June 2016	Brexit referendum. Leave won with 51.9 per cent against Remain.
24 June 2016	Resignation of David Cameron's government.
13 July 2016	Creation of Theresa May's government, including both pro-Remain and pro-Brexit Conservative ministers.
Autumn 2016	Creation of lobbying groups in the financial sector to influence the withdrawal negotiations.
2 October 2016	May announced that her government would trigger the withdrawal procedure within six months.
7 November 2016	The High Court of Justice denied the government the right to trigger the withdrawal procedure, ruling that it must be triggered by Parliament, where the majority was in favour of Remain.
24 January 2017	The Supreme Court authorised the government to trigger the withdrawal procedure.
29 March 2017	Withdrawal procedure triggered under article 50 of the European Union Treaty.
18 April 2017	May announced a snap election.
8 June 2017	Labour led by Jeremy Corbyn won numerous seats, depriving the Tory Party of its majority.
26 June 2017	The Conservative Party had to sign a coalition agreement with the DUP, a radical party with a pro-hard Brexit stance.

6 July 2018	Theresa May revealed her proposals for the withdrawal agreement, the 'Chequers plan'.
8 July 2018	Pro-hard Brexit minister David Davis resigned, followed by 17 other ministers, including Boris Johnson.
25 November 2018	First withdrawal agreement negotiated between Theresa May and the European Union. It was an ambiguous agreement, that sidestepped contentious points over the hard or soft nature of Brexit.
15 January 2019	The House of Commons rejected the agreement, with a coalition of pro-Remain and pro-hard Brexit MPs.
29 March 2019	The House of Commons rejected the agreement for the third time. The Speaker of the House invoked an antiquated rule to prevent the government from presenting the agreement a fourth time.
11 April 2019	The May government asked the European Union to postpone withdrawal. The European Union granted the request, but stipulated that the May government had to hold European elections in May 2019 as per schedule.
23 May 2019	The European elections were a defeat for the Conservative Party.
24 May 2019	Theresa May resigned.
24 July 2019	The Conservative Party designated Boris Johnson to replace May. Johnson formed a government of pro-hard Brexit ministers, but it was put in minority by Parliament from its first vote.
28 August 2019	Johnson announced the prorogation of Parliament for two months, to prevent it from voting on an eventual no-deal Brexit.
4 September 2019	Johnson excluded 21 Conservative MPs who had voted in favour of a soft Brexit and against his government.
24 September 2019	The Supreme Court annulled the prorogation of Parliament.

4 October 2019	The House of Commons forced the Johnson government to ask for a further postponement of withdrawal.
17 October 2019	The Johnson government unveiled a new withdrawal agreement very similar to the previous one except on the Northern Ireland issue.
22 October 2019	The House of Commons rejected the new agreement.
29 October 2019	Boris Johnson announced a snap election.
11 November 2019	Brexit Party president Nigel Farage announced that his party would not present candidates in constituencies held by Conservatives.
12 December 2019	The Conservative Party won the general election by a large margin.
22 January 2020	The new Parliament approved the agreement of 17 October 2019.
31 January 2020	The United Kingdom withdrew from the European Union.

Negotiations began immediately after the referendum. The Cameron government resigned on 24 June 2016 and the Conservative Party chose as its leader Theresa May, Cameron's home secretary, who had tactically decided to stay on the sidelines during the referendum campaign. The elections in the Conservative Party and in the House of Commons led to a new government on 13 July 2016 which included both pro-Remain and pro-Brexit Conservatives. As the Conservative Party was deeply split over the issue of Brexit, this coalition seemed to be a reasonable way forward in order to retain power while avoiding a general election. But behind this political division lay an economic rift in the business community that would progressively force the Conservative Party to clarify its position on Brexit and choose sides.

At the same time the economic powers involved in the debate began to organise. The rival factions of the City each put forth their claims for the post-referendum negotiations. What second-wave finance actors wanted above all was for the United Kingdom to jettison European regulations. First-wave finance wanted to find a way to retain its access to the European capital market. It quickly became evident that the political equilibrium in continental Europe would not allow the British financial markets to have it both ways – in other words, one faction of the financial sector would have to lose if the other was to win. From this point forward, the debate in the UK was centred on two main outcomes: the so-called 'soft Brexit' and 'hard Brexit' options. For the financial sector, a soft Brexit meant continued compliance with European financial regulations, in exchange for some form of passporting rights, along the lines of the equivalence regime that the European Union already had with Switzerland and which allowed Swiss financial companies to operate on EU markets without the country being a member state. Inversely, the proponents of a hard Brexit wanted the UK to be able to exempt itself from European regulation, particularly financial regulation, and this entailed accepting the loss of access to the Single Market. Not surprisingly, the large banks and conventional insurance companies supported a soft Brexit and the negotiation of an agreement that included a post-Brexit financial passport, whereas investment funds pushed for a so-called clean break with the European Union.

Preparatory manoeuvres soon began in the City. To influence the outcome of the negotiations between London and Brussels, the competing financial sectors formed lobbying groups which were as highly structured as any government embassy. On the first-wave side, the lobbying association of the City of London, called TheCityUK (initially pro-Remain, then pro-soft Brexit), created the Brexit Steering Group, led jointly by the chairman of Barclays, John McFarlane, and the chairman of the insurer Prudential plc, Paul Manduca (both of whom had been pro-Remain). These two sectors – large banks and conventional insurance companies – also set up the European Financial Services Chairmen's Advisory Committee (EFSCAC, pro-soft Brexit), which included the chairs of the four principal UK banks (Barclays, Lloyds, RBS and HSBC) and those of the main international financial institutions in London (Morgan Stanley, BNY Mellon, Santander, Aviva and Allianz). The EFSCAC had a secretariat that organised its activity according to themes related to each subsector (commercial, retail and investment banking, insurance, market infrastructure, asset management).

On the side of second-wave finance, pro-Brexit financial actors launched the Financial Services Negotiation Forum (FSN Forum) in the Autumn of 2016 to counter the influence of the EFSCAC committee. This group explicitly lobbied for a hard Brexit and sought to prod the government in the direction of what it termed 'the best alternative to a negotiated settlement position'. By this the FSN Forum meant that it sought to water down the terms of the post-Brexit deal as much as possible, and, barring a satisfactory deal, would prefer a 'no-deal' Brexit. Claiming to unite 'all the institutions not represented' by TheCityUK and the EFSCAC, the FSN Forum was presided by Anthony Belchambers, a pioneer in the derivatives sector in Europe. Politically, the FSN Forum was close to the Eurosceptic fringe of the Conservative Party and to the Global Britain think tank. Even more aggressive than the FSN Forum in its support for a hard Brexit, the Leave Means Leave group was founded at the end of 2016 by the real estate investment fund manager Richard Tice, with the moral (and financial) support of Peter Hargreaves, cited earlier in this book. Representing the most intransigent hard-Brexiters, this group was close to Nigel Farage and the Brexit Party (formerly UKIP). Its founders were nicknamed the 'bad boys of Brexit' by the press. The group called for a no-deal

Brexit, meaning that the relationship between the EU and the UK would be governed only by World Trade Organization treaties and other pre-existing conventions. Such a no-deal Brexit would have allowed the UK to pursue an aggressive policy of social, fiscal and financial dumping beyond the pale of the European Union.

After a period of several months during which the two sides gauged each other, the political situation became increasingly heated. The pro-Remainers expressed resistance when Theresa May announced the imminent triggering of the withdrawal procedure in October 2016. The neoliberal political regime of accumulation refused to go to its grave quietly. Gina Miller, a pro-Remain figure and CEO of the wealth management company SCM Direct, launched a legal procedure against May's withdrawal letter. The High Court of Justice, and then the Supreme Court, asserted that the government could not launch the withdrawal procedure without the agreement of Parliament. The Conservative and Labour leaderships both asked their respective MPs to vote in favour of triggering the withdrawal. But in a Parliament dominated by MPs who represented the interests of the old neoliberal order, a parliamentary guerrilla war quickly unfolded. Only after six months of judicial procedure and parliamentary debates was the government able to trigger the withdrawal procedure, on 29 March 2017.

This first episode foreshadowed the delicate balancing act of successive Conservative governments after March 2017. Like the business and the financial communities, the Conservative Party was deeply divided between the proponents of a hard Brexit and the advocates for a soft Brexit and Remain. From March to June 2017 Theresa May tried to deal with these contradictory tendencies. On the one side, the Conservative MPs of the European Research Group, led by hardliner and hedge fund manager Jacob Rees-Mogg, announced their rebellious intention to obtain a no-deal Brexit and reset the relationship between the European Union and the United Kingdom on World Trade Organization terms. This position was favourably received in some quarters of the government. On 9 March, Boris Johnson, then Foreign Secretary, declared with Thatcherian overtones that the UK should not pay the £50 billion 'bill' that the EU was claiming, even if it meant accepting a no-deal Brexit. On the other side, the majority of MPs, Lords and most Conservative Party staff, plus the home secretary Amber Rudd and the former prime minister John Major, pressed May to obtain a soft Brexit, or even to back out of Brexit altogether. Hobbled by her narrow parliamentary majority and these emerging divergences, May called a snap election at the end of April in the hope of strengthening her majority and her grip over the party. Far from clarifying the situation, however, the election of 8 June 2017 only worsened matters. Although the Conservatives gained voters, the Labour Party won over even more voters, and the Conservative Party lost its absolute majority in the Commons. Henceforth it was dependent on the small Northern Irish DUP to pass crucial Brexit legislation.

Initially favourable towards a soft Brexit, May progressively hardened her position under the pressure of Eurosceptic MPs.[23] Her government began to turn its back on first-wave finance, distancing itself from the large banks and insurance companies that had previously had the ear and careful attention of the Cameron government. 'They [May's ministers] refuse to hear to our concerns by choice', complained an executive in a large British bank anonymously.[24] The Brexit negotiations called into question the mechanisms that the banking and insurance lobbies customarily used to weigh in on politics. Instead of relying on the 'City-Treasury-Bank of London nexus', where UK financial regulations and the British position on financial matters in Brussels were habitually drawn up jointly by these partners,[25] May entrusted the Brexit negotiations to a new ministerial department, the Department for Exiting the European Union (DExEU). At its head she appointed David Davis, a hard-Brexiter and figure on the social right who openly disdained the interests of the banking sector. Speaking of Davis, the banker quoted above said: 'We definitely focused on the Treasury. Is it easy to get access to some of the senior people in DExEU? Probably not. Is David Davis interested in us? No. His views on the banking sector are pretty well-known.'[26]

With her majority hanging by a thread, May tried to find a path between the two opposing factions of the Conservative Party. On 6 July 2018, she outlined her plan for Brexit, the 'Chequers plan' (named after the prime minister's residence), based on the concept of 'controlled divergence' with respect to the European institutional arrangement. But this intermediate position did not suit the supporters of soft Brexit, who felt that it would lead the United Kingdom too far from the European Union. Nor did it satisfy the proponents of hard Brexit, who believed they could force a more radical break with European regulations, or even EU officials, who denounced May's proposal as a manoeuvre to 'have the cake and eat it too'. Realising that the situation was inextricable, Brexit minister David Davis resigned on 8 July, followed in the course of the summer by 17 other pro-hard Brexit ministers, including Boris Johnson. At the Salzburg summit of 21 September, the EU discredited May's plan even further when Donald Tusk, president of the European Council, observed that her proposal 'was not working', and the Brexit negotiator Michel Barnier stated that it would be 'illegal'.

Weakened by this complete absence of support, Theresa May finally struck a deal with the European Union on 25 November 2018, couched in an ambiguous document that left most points of contention unresolved. The sovereignty of the United Kingdom in regulatory matters was affirmed, but at the same time it was stated that the UK would need to cooperate with the EU in social, environmental and financial matters. Second-wave finance representatives considered this deal to be contrary to their interests. The Brexit Party MEP and real estate fund manager Richard Tice described it as the 'worst deal anyone has ever proposed in history', one that would 'trap the United Kingdom with issues like regulation, level playing field, tax'. The deal did not gain strong support from first-wave financial actors, who were concerned that it did not mention any promise of access to European capital markets for British financiers.

May nonetheless tried to get Parliament to accept the deal. Three times, on 15 January, 12 March and 19 March 2019, the House of Commons rejected the deal by a large majority. Supported by MPs, the Speaker of the House John Bercow refused to let May bring the same deal to Parliament for a fourth vote. Having already pushed back the withdrawal date a first time on 20 March 2019, May was obliged to ask the European Union for a second deadline extension. This request was granted on the condition that the United Kingdom proceed with the election of members to the European Parliament in May, as in all EU countries. Theresa May's Conservative Party was routed at the polls. It came in fifth, with only 8.8 per cent of the votes, behind the triumphant Brexit Party of Nigel Farage (30.5 per cent), the Liberal Democrats (19.6 per cent), Jeremy Corbyn's Labour Party (13.6 per cent) and the Greens (11.8 per cent). May resigned as Conservative leader.

After a short tussle for the leadership, Boris Johnson took her place and became prime minister on 24 July 2019. This did not change anything in the existing power relationships, however, as Johnson failed to unite divided business and political leaders behind him. His government found itself in the minority on the day of its first vote in Parliament. From his election as prime minister to the dissolution of Parliament on

6 November 2019, Johnson's government was in the minority on 12 bills. It managed to get a majority of votes on only two bills in the House of Commons. In August 2019, mired in the conflict between his Eurosceptic supporters and a predominantly Europhile Parliament, Johnson decided to simply shut down Parliament. He tried to prorogue it – in other words to suspend parliamentary activity during the most crucial moments of the Brexit negotiations. This triggered a deep crisis for the British neoliberal political regime of accumulation. The Speaker of the House of Commons denounced the prorogation as a 'constitutional scandal'. Commentors accused the prime minister of fomenting a 'coup'. The Supreme Court finally judged that the prorogation was 'unlawful and thus void and of no effect'. Johnson had no other choice but to accept the verdict, and Parliament reconvened the following day in Westminster.

British political institutions continued to sink deeper into crisis, with the official Brexit date looming. Johnson said that he would rather be 'dead in a ditch' than ask the European Union for another extension of the deadline, but Parliament pointedly voted to order him to ask for an extension and put the government in the minority once again. Johnson called the rebellious Conservative MPs 'traitors' who had supported the 'surrender' of the country to Brussels. The parliamentary vote did not prevent Johnson from creating doubts about his intentions. He insinuated that he might circumvent the law of the land and openly disobey Parliament. The Labour Party called for his removal, and several judges threatened to send him to jail if he refused to comply with the parliamentary injunction. In the end, on 19 October 2019, Johnson sent a letter asking the EU for an extension, but he refused to sign it and simultaneously sent a second letter asking for the shortest possible extension.

In the midst of this regime crisis, Boris Johnson's government was hanging by a thread, and a crucial one indeed: the support of the advocates of hard Brexit and their powerful second-wave finance backers was weakening. This was underscored by acrimonious debates within the Conservative Party. The former Chancellor of the Exchequer Philip Hammond directly linked the prime minister's defence of a no-deal Brexit to the support that Johnson had from hedge fund managers, explaining that the latter had backed Johnson in the hope that a no-deal exit would make their bet on a fall of the pound profitable. Even the prime minister's sister, Rachel Johnson, declared on Sky News in September 2019 that her brother's position was in her view influenced by the interests of his financial supporters. The argument that second-wave financial actors sought a no-deal Brexit to make a money on the fall of the pound did not, however, stand up under close examination. Indeed, hedge fund manager Crispin Odey explained to the *Financial Times* that he was targeting something far bigger with his support, including 'reforming the constitution' and shaking up 'the deep state'.[27] As the situation worsened, and despite the emphasis that was put on the whimsical character of its leader, the Johnson government increasingly looked like what it really was: a government of the pro-hard Brexit factions of the financial sector. To paraphrase Marx, only an exceptional division between the factions of the financial sector could 'create the strange circumstances and relationships that made it possible for a grotesque and mediocre personality to play a hero's part'.[28]

His strategies for bypassing Parliament having failed, Boris Johnson had no other solution but to dissolve Parliament and call a snap election. He asked MPs to vote for dissolution on 29 October 2019. He then engaged in a series of brutal purges within the ranks of the Conservative Party, to consolidate the ideas and people preferred by second-wave finance. Reorganised around hard-Brexiters, the party engaged in the election campaign. Pro-Brexit forces converged behind it. Farage announced that his Brexit Party would not field candidates in constituencies held by Conservatives. The Brexit forces raised much more campaign money than their opponents. The Conservatives and the Brexit Party together raised £14.7 million, compared to £4.2 million for Labour. The Labour Party was itself paralysed at the time by an internal stand-off between its neoliberal, pro-Remain centrist wing, and its socialist Eurosceptical left wing. The Conservatives won the election, giving a broad majority to Johnson's second government.

As a sign of the times, second-wave finance executives began to set up in Westminster. The new Johnson government marked the moment when former members of these financial subsectors rose to the highest level of British politics. Traditional financial sectors were still hanging on to the access to government circles that had been their privilege for three decades. At the beginning of 2020, Andrea Leadsom, a former investment banker at Barclays, was Secretary of State for Business, Energy and Industrial Strategy, and Sajid Javid, a former investment banker at Deutsche Bank, was Chancellor of the Exchequer. Both ministers were removed in February 2020. Traditional finance was now rivalled by the voices of new financial sectors. Jacob Rees-Mogg was a partner of the hedge fund Somerset Capital and the leader of the Eurosceptic European Research Group in the House of Commons. He was designated as Leader of the House of Commons by Johnson, rewarding his stance in favour of a hard Brexit and the role he played in weakening Theresa May. Rishi Sunak, a hedge fund manager at The Children's Investment Fund (TCI) and a supporter of Johnson, replaced Sajid Javid as Chancellor of the Exchequer in February 2020.

At this time, Boris Johnson's government and its supporters came to dominate British institutions. The new Parliament finally approved the withdrawal agreement on 22 January 2020, and the United Kingdom left the European Union on 31 January. Theresa May's proposed agreement had been rejected in November 2018 and Boris Johnson's proposal was accepted in January 2020.[29] In the intervening 14 months the House of Commons was twice dissolved, major political personalities were consigned to oblivion, former hedge fund executives replaced former investment bankers in the government, Conservative rebels opposed to the new order were excluded, and significant portions of British parliamentary and constitutional law were rewritten. And this was only the beginning. Once the ruins of the neoliberal regime of accumulation had been swept away, there was still a lot to be done to build a new regime of accumulation and construct an institutional arrangement to channel capital to the rising financial class.

First came the task of setting up a political regime favourable to the new financial capitalism. Just after the December 2019 election victory, Dominic Cummings, then special advisor to Boris Johnson, went about the business of reforming the British technostructure and transforming the civil service. He was later dropped by Johnson after being tarred by a scandal, but Michael Gove, as Chancellor of the Duchy of Lancaster, took over the reform mission. The second task was to construct a new institutional arrangement that would guarantee high profits to second-wave financial actors. The latter were no longer content to thrive on the margins of an arrangement favourable to their first-wave finance competitors. They now wanted solid and long-lasting institutional guarantees to protect their activity. The British government clarified its agenda: it opted to diverge from European regulations and accept the loss of access to the Single Market, giving preference to second-wave finance over the first-wave. On 24 January 2020, the Chancellor of the Exchequer explained the British position: 'There will not be alignment, we will not be a rule-taker, we will not be in the single market and we will not be in the customs union – and we will do this by the end of the year.' With this break from the European political regime of accumulation the government could begin to establish the institutional arrangement that would guarantee profitability for its supporters.

The struggle we have described did not end on the day of the British exit from the European Union. Conflicts between first- and second-wave financial actors continued to grip the City and frame discussions with financial regulators in the UK. Although the withdrawal agreement was very favourable to second-wave finance actors, as it gave British authorities the right to potentially engage in fiscal and financial dumping, the Johnson government was careful to strike a balance between the old neoliberal institutions and the new libertarian-authoritarian entities. It did not engage in significant deregulation, despite the launch of free ports; it even raised corporate taxes and pledged to achieve net zero carbon emissions by 2050. After having donated to many campaigns and even to the refurbishment of the prime minister's flat (funds provided by private equity fund manager and Conservative donor David Brownlow), second-wave finance donors increasingly expressed their discontent with the governmental line.[30] The conflict within the financial sector also continued to ripple through the British political regime. Despite the purges of 2019, the Conservative Party remained deeply divided. Some libertarian Conservatives eager for a 'Singapore-on-Thames' were disappointed by the overly timid post-Brexit reforms, while others were irritated by Johnson's vocal conversion to ambitious carbon targets.[31] This resulted in constant battles in and around the Johnson government and paved the way for potential future regime crises.

In the past five decades British capitalism has gone through three successive political regimes of accumulation, each corresponding to a specific configuration of the financial sector. It was initially organised around a Fordist regime, with a strongly redistributive welfare state and a financial sector dominated by banks. Next came a financialised regime based on a regulatory state, in which finance was mostly concentrated in stock markets. Today we see the emergence of a new financialised regime, based on an increasingly authoritarian state: social and civil rights are restricted and alternative financial actors are able to make a profit in markets that were not financialised up to now. The new political regime of accumulation has not mechanically followed the rise in power of second-wave finance. A patient effort was needed to build a coalition of political interests, resolve institutional power struggles, and spread the new shared ideology, in order to turn the neoliberal regime into a libertarian-authoritarian one. This shift began in Britain at the same time as similar shifts in the United States and Brazil, with immediate consequences for other European countries. The change has strengthened second-wave financial actors in the UK, and they are beginning to dream of a more favourable political regime. It has weakened the neoliberal edifice at the heart of the European Union and put pressure on governments who, despite having the support of first-wave financial actors, are now asked to comply with the economic interests of alternative finance.

3

From European Neoliberalism to Authoritarian Libertarianism

European neoliberalism is in crisis. Under this political regime of accumulation governments accord moderate civil rights to citizens, and are aligned with the economic orientations of the so-called 'Washington consensus'. This regime is now shaky. The democratic and technocratic national and regional institutions that ensured the fortunes of first-wave finance are slowly crumbling. They have been undermined by the recent aggressive intrusion of financial operators who are determined to make their voice heard in institutional discussions. A sign of these actors' newly acquired political strength is that they are in a position to attack the European Union, one of the main institutions of neoliberalism, and to reshape capitalist institutions to tailor them to their own economic interests. The neoliberal capitalism of the last four decades has become a kind of 'late capitalism'.[1] The contours of this degraded neoliberalism are still blurry. The declining dominant forces are losing ground, but the rising ones, who are busy weakening neoliberal institutions, have not yet fully occupied the territory.

Is leaving the European Union the way to get rid of neoliberalism?

The political regime of accumulation that British second-wave finance is trying to build has one obvious characteristic: it is constructed in opposition to the European Union (other characteristics are discussed later in this chapter). This does not mean that the new regime espouses autarchic or absolutist rule, or that it rejects any form of international cooperation. Rather, it signifies that it is in conflict specifically with the neoliberal modes of cooperation between states. The relationship of the new regime of accumulation with the existing neoliberal model deserves attention because it contradicts views that have become dominant in political and academic critical thought.

It is worth noting that the notion that the European Union 'constitutionalises' neoliberalism took hold at a specific moment in history.[2] It emerged when Syriza – a coalition of left and far-left movements founded in 2004 – came to power in Greece in the wake of the European public debt crisis. How did this historical event produce this assessment of the European Union? In the snap election of 6 May 2012 Syriza recorded the best electoral score of its history with 16.8 per cent of the vote. The coalition became the second-ranking political force in the country. At the time, Europe was still shaken by the fallout from the 2008 economic crisis, and a majority of member states were governed by Conservative leaders (Angela Merkel in Germany, David Cameron in the United Kingdom, Nicolas Sarkozy in France, Mariano Rajoy in Spain, Mario Monti in Italy). Syriza's unexpected success gave hope to social-democratic and anti-capitalist movements in Europe. Greece was at the time targeted by yet another so-called assistance memorandum from the European Central Bank (ECB) and the International Monetary Fund (IMF). The memorandum and its injunctions forced the country to reimburse its debtors and institute a new set of severe economic reforms. In Greece as in other parts of Europe under similar pressure, the imposed austerity regime ruined the country, inequalities grew and the people became increasingly angry. For the first time since the 2008 crisis, Alexis Tsipras, the leader of Syriza, was on the threshold of power. Hostile to the austerity policy, he had declared in reference to the memorandum negotiations: 'you don't negotiate with hell'. After 30 years of neoliberal policies and fiscal discipline, left-wing analysts rejoiced at the prospect of a government that would refuse the golden rule of the 3 per cent maximum deficit imposed by the Maastricht treaty, that would refuse the new wave of privatisations stipulated by the memorandum, and that, if it were joined by similar forces in Europe, could pave the way for a truly social Europe.

In May 2012 Tsipras toured Europe. In France he met the leaders of the Front de gauche, Jean-Luc Mélenchon and Pierre Laurent, and held a press conference with them at the National Assembly. In Germany, he had talks with Die Linke's leader, Oskar Lafontaine. He invited Pablo Iglesias, general secretary of the Spanish party Podemos, to Athens. Summarising a widespread view in southern European left-wing parties, Iglesias declared that 'in Europe, [...] our countries have become quasi-protectorates, new colonies where powerful unelected people are destroying our social rights and threaten the social and political cohesion of our societies'.[3] It looked like the anti-austerity left in Europe would at last be able to come together and gain traction. Continuing this movement, in September 2015 Jeremy Corbyn took the leadership of the Labour Party. Tsipras hailed Corbyn's victory, saying that it 'strengthened the European front against austerity and sent a message of hope'. People had struggled unsuccessfully against austerity policies in the streets, but they had managed to block them through elections. At the January 2015 general election in Greece, Syriza took 36.3 per cent of the vote and sent 149 MPs (out of 300 seats) to the Parliament. Addressing a jubilant crowd, Tsipras triumphantly announced that 'Greece is entering a new era. It leaves behind a catastrophic era of austerity, fear, autocracy. It leaves behind five years of humil iation and suffering.' Tsipras immediately acted to renegotiate the Greek debt. Despite the clearly expressed popular will, the Troika (as the three-pronged force of the ECB, the European Commission and the IMF was called) made no concessions. Five months later, Tsipras decided to break off the talks and at one o'clock in the morning on 27 June 2015 he announced that he would hold a referendum, taking the Troika by surprise:

> We have been battling under the astonishing, constant threat of financial strangulation [...] We have been asked to apply the memorandum policies in the exact same way as our predecessors [...] These proposals absolutely violate the European *acquis*. Their goal is to humiliate a whole people [...] Our responsibility is to answer to the ultimatum by appealing to the will of the Greek people [...] Greece, the country where democracy was born, should send to the world a resoundingly democratic message. I pledge myself to respect the result of the referendum, whatever it is.

As Athens was at risk of default as early as 30 June, the Troika had offered a €12 billion loan to be paid out in four instalments by the end of November, in exchange for austerity reforms that, in Tsipras's, words 'undermine[ed] the revival of the Greek economy and society'. This was the Troika proposal that Tsipras wanted the Greek people to vote on. All over Europe, *oxi* ('no') became the watchword for the left, and 61.3 per cent of Greek voters rejected the memorandum on 6 July 2015.

The Troika immediately declared that it did not intend to respect the will of the Greek voters. Wolfgang Schäuble, the German finance minister, brutally put on the table the issue of 'Grexit'. Jean-Claude Juncker, the president of the European Commission, declared that 'there can be no democratic choice against European treaties'.[4] Tsipras had no choice but to break with the EU. Against all odds he rejected this course of action. On 13 July 2015 he signed an agreement that imposed new austerity measures and privatisations on the country in exchange for additional loans in the coming months. His finance minister Yanis Varoufakis resigned and one month later Tsipras announced his own resignation.

It was at this moment that the European Union came to be analysed as a structurally neoliberal institution, constitutionally protected from any form of popular influence. Exit from the EU became a shared objective for an increasing number of organisations opposed to neoliberal policies. This stance derived from the conclusion that if the leader of a radical left organisation, strongly supported by his people in street demonstrations, in elections and in Parliament, had failed to reform the Union, then it was probably not possible to change it at all. On 19 January 2015, the French left-wing intellectual Frédéric Lordon wrote:

> The alternative for Syriza is very simple: either accept European demands or throw them out altogether. But there will be no third way. And if Tsipras believes that he will be able to stay in the euro and get more than bags of peanuts, he is lying to himself. [...] There is only one thing to do: remind Syriza of the considerable responsibility it now has: to truly contest austerity in the only possible way, *by breaking out*.[5]

In the same fashion, critical economist Cédric Durand also wrote that 'getting out of the euro is essential to a left-wing strategy'. The events of 13 July 2015 were 'haunting' him, as well as a growing number of heterodox European economists, sociologists and political scientists. Referring to Tsipras' acceptance of the Troika's conditions, Durand wrote: 'This morning, when the hopes of millions of Greeks have suddenly vanished, revealed a cruel strategic impasse: if the left continues to prioritise the European ideal, then it will be doomed to negate itself when reaching power.'[6] Some on the left began to explore the prospect of an exit from the European Union. Several leaders met in Paris in November 2015, including Oskar Lafontaine (Germany), Jean-Luc Mélenchon (France), Stefano Fassina (Italy), Zoé Konstantopoulo and Yanis Varoufakis (Greece). This was called the 'Plan B summit', a meeting held to draft an exit scenario. The Greek experience had shaped a clear and common understanding of the situation in the mid-2010s. On one side were the defenders of Europe and neoliberalism, signifying constitutional protection of the rights of financial capital and the end of popular sovereignty. On the other side were those willing to break with the European Union, reset the balance between the rights of labour and of capital, and build back the regulatory and redistributive state.

This analysis was shared by a portion of the non-neoliberal British left. In 2016 the Brexit referendum did not generate enormous enthusiasm in the Labour Party. Centre-left Labour leaders, who accepted the legacy of Tony Blair's New Labour, defended Remain. But many others, on the left of the party, refused to support Remain and even called for what they called Lexit (a Left Brexit). The British left found itself divided between explicit supporters of Brexit and Remainers favourable to 'another Europe'. On the Leave side were the militants of the Socialist Workers Party (SWP), the Socialist Party, the Communist Party of Britain, and the communist newspaper *Morning Star*, which launched the official Lexit campaign on 13 April 2016. On the Remain side were not only New Labour centrists, but also figures on the radical left who had joined Yanis Varoufakis's movement, Another Europe Is Possible. These included, for instance, Jeremy Corbyn's shadow Chancellor of the Exchequer, John McDonnell, film director Ken Loach, Green MP Caroline Lucas and Momentum leader

Michael Chessum. Under the combined pressure of his party's right-wing and this movement for another Europe, Corbyn, who had consistently opposed British membership of the EEC and EU since 1975, accepted officially supporting Remain, but abstained from campaigning and even criticised the 'failed neoliberal policies' of the European Union a few days before the referendum.

These political and academic thinkers critical of neoliberalism are not alone in considering the European construction as a process that constitutionalises neoliberal policies. Friedrich Hayek wrote as early as 1939 that 'there would have to be less government all round if [a European] federation is to be practicable', and this federation would be synonymous with an inevitable liberalisation of goods and capital markets.[7] In the late 1960s and 1970s, two Marxist thinkers, Ernest Mandel and Nicos Poulantzas, also reflected on the nature of the European construction. For Mandel, it was the domination of US capital that was forcing national European capitalists to coalesce in a single regional entity. For Poulantzas, this analysis replicated the myth of a 'united Europe', whereas 'the structure of domination and dependency of the imperialist chain was organising uneven relationships, even between social bodies at the centre', that is to say between European countries themselves.[8] Despite these points of disagreement, both advocates and critics of socialism shared a common vision of the European construction: it was a way to protect the European capitalist order against the socialist threat.[9]

Since the mid-2000s this approach to the European Union has been supported by a growing body of critical work. The European construction has frequently been described as an undertaking meant to stifle democratic deliberation and 'make European societies surrender to the process of capital accumulation'.[10] In their book *The Social Europe Will Never Exist*, François Denord and Antoine Schwartz write that 'the

pro-business, free-market orientation of the European construction [...] did not result from historical contingencies' but
was an inherent part of the European project itself.[11] Wolfgang
Streeck has also shown how the European Union subjected
member states to 'fiscal consolidation and debt discipline
policies' in order 'to reassure the financial markets that in case
of doubt their claims can and will have priority over those of
citizens'.[12] This institutional construction would replace the
traditional duty of the state, the 'duty to protect' (the people),
with the 'duty to pay' (the financial markets).

The European Union has been construed as a powerful
engine to counter 'the intrusion of masses in the capitalist
relationship'.[13] The EU does not embody the progressive
broadening of citizenship from national citizenship to an
eventual European citizenship. Rather, it has confiscated all
forms of citizenship, understood as the ability to take part in
decisions of political sovereignty. Frédéric Lordon analyses
the European construction as a step by which 'sovereign
states, by themselves, freely and deliberately organised the
institutional arrangement that diminished their own sovereignty'.[14] To what end? 'To make way for the power of private
capital.'[15] The European Union is a regional instrument to
achieve free-market globalisation and consequently is in
head-on conflict with the exercise of political sovereignty, that
is to say with democracy. The EU has integrated states within
a supranational system of institutions shielded from electoral
pressures; it has isolated pro-market policies from democratic
influence in most circumstances, and simultaneously provided
an easy-to-use justification to national governments who seek
to enact unpopular neoliberal reforms: the European Union
demands it, the European Union imposes it, and we can only
consent to what the European Union wants.

On this view, the powerlessness of European states was
deliberately organised by those who nominally deplored it. In

this respect, the EU is a convenient institutional alternative to explicit authoritarianism in the face of social movements provoked by the opportunities for ever greater capital accumulation granted to the dominant classes. Rather than using police force against the people, as anticipated by Rosa Luxemburg, the dominant classes have created technical and constitutional shields to prevent the people from taking part in economic decisions.[16] In the end, European integration is a clever institutional innovation which conceals the beneficiaries of accumulation, prevents any form of contestation, and legitimates the disempowerment of the people and submission to the power of markets.

On 23 June 2016, the Brexit event turned these analyses on their head. The referendum revealed that exiting the European Union could serve political aims very different from those of the anti-neoliberal left. The EU was indeed the ideal neoliberal institution, but those who defend the right to accumulate wealth intended to go even further. The EU had been the privileged political regime of accumulation for many financial sectors for over 40 years, and had fostered the financialisation of European economies and the enrichment of the possessors of capital. Suddenly, new financial actors envisioned an alternative institutional architecture posited on a break with the European Union. In their eyes, getting out of the EU offered the prospect of a new wave of deregulation, never mind a broader increase in social inequalities and a radical overhaul of civil rights. The EU had enabled the UK to coalesce with other European states behind the hegemony of the United States, to safeguard the neoliberal economic framework and to reduce the sovereignty of the people all over Europe. But now the proponents of second-wave finance felt that it was outside of the EU that they could best pursue their favoured economic and social policies.

This was plainly visible in the arguments developed by Conservative pro-Brexit think tanks. The UK had entered the EEC to defend alignment with the United States, but the federalist tendencies displayed by the Franco-German coalition within the bloc quickly irritated British advocates of the transatlantic alliance. During the 2000s, they began to dream of a Global Britain that would be open not only to Europe but also to the rest of the world, especially the US and the Commonwealth. For some financial sectors the turn had already been taken at the time the referendum debate began. Of £20.1 billion of insurance and pension fund services exported by the United Kingdom, only 12 per cent were exported to the European Union, compared with 46 per cent to the United States and 42 per cent to the rest of the world.[17] The Eurosceptic Conservative think tank Global Britain published a document entitled 'Why Our Financial Services Need a Clean Brexit' in the Autumn of 2016. The authors urged the British financial sector to reassert its international scope by strengthening its ties with Asia, the United States and Commonwealth countries, where growth rates offered the prospect of juicy market shares in the future. At stake was an opportunity for the UK to deepen its 'special relationship' with the United States and to join forces with the emerging new international order. The United States had long supported the construction of powerful regional organisations, initially as a bulwark against communist expansion and then later as a means to institutionalise the free circulation of capital all over the world. This stance began to change in 2010. From then on the United States sought to curb the power of these organisations to impose constraints on free competition. To integrate into this new international order, the United Kingdom had to leave the EU.

Brexit was also understood by the new financial entities as a unique opportunity to renegotiate the British social contract on a basis more favourable to their interests. Brexit clearly strengthened centrifugal forces within the United Kingdom: Northern Ireland and Scotland voted massively in favour of Remain. For these countries, membership in the European Union was a powerful driver of their commitment to the United Kingdom. To put it bluntly, without the EU, why stay in the UK? On 24 June 2016, Nicola Sturgeon, the Scottish first minister, called for a new referendum on independence for Scotland. Likewise, the Republican party Sinn Féin asked to hold the reunification poll provided for in the Irish peace agreement of 1998. The threat of the dissolution of the United Kingdom did not frighten London financial circles. These last remaining vestiges of empire were costly to them. First of all, Scotland and Northern Ireland had the unfortunate habit of sending left-wing MPs to Westminster at each general election. In addition these two nations received significant fiscal transfers that made it harder for England (and London) to become a tax haven. Recent calculations showed that if Northern Ireland and Scotland were independent states, in 2016 their budget deficits would have amounted to respectively 29 per cent and 12.5 per cent of their GDP. In the same year, the budget surplus of London alone was equivalent to the fiscal transfers absorbed by these lower income countries of the United Kingdom; without these last remains of empire the net tax levies on the City would be significantly lower. Public positions in favour of the 'independence of England' from the poorer nations of the United Kingdom emerged during the Scottish referendum debate of 2014. Nicholas Shaxson, a specialist on tax evasion practices in the United Kingdom and member of the Tax Justice Network, explained during the 2014 debate that 'a reduction in the UK population would lessen democratic pressures, somewhat, and make the UK look still more like a tax haven than it already is'.[18] For a long time UKIP had been calling for a decrease in fiscal transfers and an increase in the autonomy of England. 'The English people', said Nigel Farage, 'had been suckers for too long' and English taxes were 'inordinately' benefiting Scotland.

Here we can see how the break with the regional institutional framework of the European Union was not envisioned to serve an emancipatory project that would entail the working class taking back control of the institutions that regulate social life. Frédéric Lordon, quoted above, wrote that 'getting back to national economic policies (which does not mean that we should stop deepening extra-economic links between countries) seemed to be the best option to reset Europe in a way that it would not be odious to its peoples'.[19] But for second-wave finance, getting back to national economic policies was thought of as the best way to get rid of all forms of regulation of social life that would prevent accumulation. Replacing the undemocratic institutions of a given country with national sovereignty seems a good idea in the abstract, but what if the country came to be dominated by what Brett Christophers calls a 'rentier economy'?[20] And what if this change ensconced the rentier core (London) even more firmly at the political centre of the economy for the future? Far from benefiting the working class, this restored national sovereignty, equated increasingly with the sovereignty of England (and hence London), served the capitalist interests of the dominant groups who coalesced behind Brexit.

Since the 1980s, European policies had encouraged the financialisation of Europe under the domination of the London financial markets, but pro-Brexit financiers now believed that the extension of their accumulation opportunities required leaving the European Union. In short, they hoped to turn London into a kind of offshore global centre – a vision nicknamed 'Singapore-on-Thames' by the media. The OECD itself worried that the 'aggressive fiscal policy' envisioned by the British government would turn the country into yet another 'tax haven'. The Singapore-on-Thames project was defended by the pro-Brexit think tanks that embodied the interest of financial circles. The Adam Smith Institute, a think tank promoting 'free markets', proposed to 'unleash the competitive potential' of the country by creating free ports, warehouses where valuable objects and artworks are domiciled to avoid taxation of any sort, on the model of Singapore and Luxembourg free ports. The Global Britain think tank also called for increasing the capacity of the London financial centre to compete with New York, Singapore and Hong Kong and make it into 'the most sensibly regulated, lowly taxed financial centre in the world'.

Capitalist actors too were keen to leave Europe – and they did not want to give power back to the working class. In this respect Brexit reveals that the issue of popular sovereignty cannot be reduced to the scale (national or European) at which it is exercised. It is quite possible to imagine mechanisms that guarantee (or confiscate) the sovereign power of the European people to make the main social and economic decisions that affect their lives. Likewise, measures to augment the right of financial accumulation can be organised either at the European or national scale. The institutional arrangements to be secured depend on the concrete and ever-changing modalities of accumulation, and the competition among the possessors of capital themselves. In good materialist logic, the grounding of institutional ruptures is to be found in the reconfiguration of these powerful economic interests. The European construction has fuelled the development of European financial sectors in past decades, but the pursuit of pro-capital policies to allow their continued expansion now involves, at least for some interests, jettisoning this obsolete institutional architecture. What are the features of the new regime of accumulation sought by European secessionists? What do these new financial actors want that the European Union cannot give them? What world are they trying to create?

The political horizon of authoritarian libertarianism

The political aims of second-wave finance are not easily elucidated. The actors in this sector rarely express themselves in public and are accustomed to doing business outside of the glare of media spotlights. Typically, our understanding of what they do not want, or rather what they *no longer* want, i.e. the European Union, has not been obtained by listening to their discourse but by following the money they are ready to spend to defend their preference. Of course, there is no election to decide which of the political regimes of accumulation imagined by factions of the business community will prevail, and there is no Electoral Commission to account for all the money spent to promote economic and political beliefs. We therefore have to sketch an outline of this political project on the basis of signs and clues found in diverse sources. We rely on the interviews that financial tycoons occasionally give to the press, publicly available data on their personal background and careers, and their affiliations with clubs, think tanks and other lobbying associations. This empirical material is scarce, but when assembled these elements reveal a consistent vision for the future world.

Paying out money to influence elections does not suffice to overthrow a political regime. To preserve and further their economic interests in an institutional arrangement that sustains their domination, emerging financial actors also have to invest in ideas. As they accumulate capital, not only do they create lobbying groups and political organisations that defend their political options, they also fund a broad network of intellectuals and think tanks. Throughout the 2000s, these intellectual organisations distilled the ideas that have accompanied the rise to financial and political power of second-wave finance. These entities are also places where economic actors who back the new political regime of accumulation forge ties and build coalitions. Their lists of board members and funding sources show that they represent the interests of second-wave finance, as well as those of other economic sectors (among them the construction, fossil fuel and tobacco industries). For such coalitions to emerge, the economic interests of their various members have to be reconciled, coordinated and collectively defended. This is the role of dedicated intellectual organisations.

These think tanks follow a consistent ideological agenda. They are commonly designated as 'Tufton Street' think tanks, referring to the street in Westminster where most of them have their headquarters. The Adam Smith Institute, the TaxPayers' Alliance, Leave Means Leave, the Global Warming Policy Foundation, the Centre for Policy Studies and the Institute of Economic Affairs all have (or had: the IEA moved recently) addresses between 55 and 57 Tufton Street. This is not just a British network: Tufton Street is integrated in the transatlantic Atlas Foundation network of think tanks. The Atlas Foundation was created in 1981 by Anthony Fisher, then a Professor at the London School of Economics (LSE), close to Friedrich Hayek, and also the founder of the Institute of Economic Affairs. This network has its own quarterly magazine, *Freedom's Champion*, and holds an annual conference called the Liberty Forums. Some 400 think tanks are members of the Atlas Foundation, most of them Anglo-American; they form a politically cohesive galaxy characterised by its libertarianism and its connections with the alt-right in the United States and with the radical fringes of the British Conservative Party. All the think tanks described below are members of the Atlas Foundation. The most emblematic members of this network in the United States are the Cato Institute funded by the Koch brothers, fossil fuel billionaires known for their denial of climate change and their libertarian opinions, and the Heritage

Foundation, also a climate-change denying, libertarian and neoconservative group.

These radical right-wing think tanks consolidate a set of ideas that constitute the political aims of second-wave finance: libertarianism, pursuit of the Thatcherian legacy, Euroscepticism, Atlanticism, authoritarianism and denial of climate change. The Tufton Street galaxy is funded by emblematic backers of the Leave victory: the founder of the hedge fund CQS Michael Hintze, the construction tycoons Lord Anthony Bamford and Malcolm McAlpine, the business partner of Arron Banks and manager of offshore financial companies Jim Mellon, and the founder of the financial derivative trading platform Stuart Wheeler. Table 17 below lists the most emblematic right-wing think tanks, the main ideas they champion and their links with British financial and political circles.

The Brexit project is not grounded in the neoliberal ideas that underpin the European construction, but rather in the libertarian ideology that permeates Tufton Street think tanks. Libertarianism can be described as an economic doctrine that aims to limit all forms of state intervention beyond the guarantee of private property against collectivism and statism.[21] It proclaims an entirely deregulated capitalist model as the sole desirable social system, a system founded on the recognition and protection of the rights of individuals, and which, consequently, bans all form of coercion in social relationships.[22] It aims to found social life exclusively on the moral, political and economic sovereignty of individuals. Chris Hattingh, a researcher at the Free Market Foundation, a libertarian think tank founded in 1975, wrote in December 2018 that 'granting people freedom to trade is radical. Allowing new businesses to sprout, free from regulations, is radical. Recognising people as diverse individuals, able to pursue their own happiness as defined by themselves, is radical.'[23] It is sometimes hard to draw the line between libertarianism and neoliberalism; the thinking of the neoliberal economist Friedrich Hayek grew more radical over time and took a libertarian direction, on the denationalisation of currencies, for instance.[24] Libertarianism remains relevant today. Libertarians go further than neoliberals regarding the reduction of the role of the state,

> because they argue that we should privatise not only education and the production of some infrastructure such as transport, but also sovereign functions. David Friedman, the son of Milton, proposes to privatise police, justice and defence. The anarcho-capitalist movement envisions the total elimination of the state with the privatisation of all its functions, including those that Adam Smith had identified as necessary state services: the army, the police and the judiciary system.[25]

With respect to Brexit, this ideology pertains to the relationship between states. Libertarian Brexiters take isolationist but not protectionist positions. The rejection of state regulation for internal matters is mirrored by the rejection of any institutional form of interstate relationships, which are to be shaped by states themselves when they contract trade agreements that match their economic interests.

Libertarianism does not offer any systematic articulation between individual actions and the common good. The liberalism of Adam Smith was a reflection on how the aggregation of individual interests, framed by laws democratically voted for by sovereign individuals, could lead to a defence of the general interest.[26] The neoliberalism of Friedrich Hayek, Milton Friedman and Ludwig von Mises considers the common good to be an object for economics, not political theory, but these thinkers maintained the focus on the common good in their economic doctrine. The radical defence of private property and the freedom to accumulate was supposed to lead to a general increase in wealth and, subsequently, social progress. The singular feature of libertarianism is that it defends an ethical approach to liberty without any regard for its effects on the common good. In this view it is fair and desirable to hold liberty above all other considerations, whatever the consequences. The justification for laissez-faire capitalism is that it is the only system compatible with this libertarian ethic, and not that this form of capitalism is socially superior, or that it would produce more wealth than alternative modes of production. Unlike liberals and neoliberals, who adopt a consequentialist approach, libertarians have a deontological approach to liberty: the freedom to accumulate is a desirable outcome in itself.[27]

The new political regime of accumulation has donned the garb of libertarian economic thought, but it is authoritarian in its political and social action. As second-wave finance is hostile to all redistributive mechanisms that guarantee the elementary conditions of existence for the population (health, education, social safety net), this regime deploys the repression of social movements and the curtailment of civil rights as privileged instruments to enforce a new social order, mainly by reinforcing controls over freedom of speech and the circulation of individuals.

From the 1980s to the 2010s, the neoliberalisation movement promoted successively by Thatcherian Conservatives, New Labour and the pro-austerity Conservatives led by David Cameron, fostered considerable expansion of the financial sector and a corresponding diminution of public services and social solidarity. The United Kingdom has become the most inegalitarian country in Western Europe, with a Gini coefficient of 34.2, 320,000 homeless people in 2018 and 20 per cent of its population in relative poverty.[28] In the same period the share of the top 1 per cent of the highest income households

Table 17 Overview of Pro-Brexit Think Tanks

Name	Date of creation	Founders	Political goal	Position on climate change	Position on Brexit	Other political positions	Support from the financial sector	Other known support	Ties with political circles
Institute of Economic Affairs (IEA)	1955	Libertarian economist Anthony Fisher, with the support of Friedrich Hayek	'Expounding the role of markets in solving economic and social problems'	Favourable to fracking and the oil industry, and to a tougher repression of environmental movements such as Extinction Rebellion	Pro-hard Brexit	Against the 'NHS religion'; explicitly libertarian	Hedge fund managers Sir Michael Hintze (CQS) and Neil Record (Record Currency Management)	Tobacco and oil companies (Philip Morris, British American Tobacco, Exxon Mobil)	Claims to have '14 alumni' within the Johnson government, including Sajid Javid, Dominic Raab, and Priti Patel
Legatum Institute (LI)	2009	Hedge fund manager Christopher Chandler, nicknamed the 'disaster capitalist' by the press	'Create the pathways from poverty to prosperity, by fostering Open Economies, Inclusive Societies and Empowered People'	Promotes contraception as a solution for climate change	Pro-hard Brexit from 2016	Promotes social and environmental deregulation; Atlanticist	The think tank emanates from its founder's hedge fund Legatum Capital, which specialises in countries and sectors hit by crises	Fossil fuel tycoon Charles Koch	Former LI president Shanker Singham (who then worked at IEA) has also been a close advisor to Boris Johnson, Michael Gove, Liam Fox and David Davis

Name	Date of creation	Founders	Political goal	Position on climate change	Position on Brexit	Other political positions	Support from the financial sector	Other known support	Ties with political circles
Initiative for Free Trade (IFT)	2017	The European MP and cofounder of Vote Leave Daniel Hannan	Defends the 'moral case for a free market'	Promotes adapting to climate change, rather than preventing it	Describes Brexit as a 'unique opportunity to revitalise the world trading system'		Venture capital fund manager Jon Moynihan (Ipex Capital) and the manager of uranium mines and offshore financial companies Jim Mellon (a partner of Arron Banks)	Cato Institute, think tank of the Koch brothers, known for denial of climate change	IFT events have welcomed Boris Johnson, Liam Fox, Michael Gove, David Gauke, Jorge Quiroga (Bolivia president), Tony Abbott (Australian prime minister), José-María Aznar (Spanish prime minister)
TaxPayers' Alliance (TPA)	2004	Hedge fund manager and Vote Leave cofounder Matthew Elliott (Shore Capital) and consultant Andrew Allum (LEK Consulting)	'Axe the tax'	Opposition to environmental taxation and to the European market for carbon emissions	Pro-hard Brexit and Eurosceptical from the start	Promotes massive privatisations, the flat tax and the end of the corporate tax; supports the US Tea Party	Funded by Stuart Wheeler, the founder of a platform for financial derivatives trading	Funded by construction tycoons Malcolm McAlpine (SR McAlpine) and Anthony Bamford (JC Bamford)	

Name	Date of creation	Founders	Political/goal	Position on climate change	Position on Brexit	Other political positions	Support from the financial sector	Other known support	Ties with political circles
Adam Smith Institute (ASI)	1977	Madsen Pirie, who quoted among his intellectual references Margaret Thatcher, Milton Friedman, Friedrich Hayek and the far-right Conservative Enoch Powell	'To defend freedom', by 'fighting big government'; the think tank describes itself as promoting 'free-market, neoliberal research'	States that climate change will be less awful than the scientific consensus is forecasting; promotes technological and market solutions to solve climate change	No official position before the referendum, despite the fact that both its director and president supported Brexit; ASI wants Brexit to 'advance the case for free trade'	Defends a system of privatisation (with publicly funded vouchers) of schools and the NHS; pro-immigration; defends the flat tax and a radical lowering of taxes; described itself as libertarian until 2016, when it referred to itself as 'neoliberal'	After the 2008 crisis, ASI issued a series of publications to promote the role of private equity and hedge funds in the economy	Tobacco industry, US libertarian think tanks, Charles Koch	In 2019 ASI's director for public affairs was recruited as Liz Truss's special advisor for foreign trade
Centre for Policy Studies (CPS)	1974	Sir Keith Joseph (a Conservative politician), Alfred Sherman (an advisor to Margaret Thatcher) and Margaret Thatcher herself	'Develop a new generation of conservative thinking, built around promoting enterprise, ownership and prosperity'; defends Margaret Thatcher's legacy	Questions the independence of the IPCC	Defends an aggressive dumping policy after Brexit, namely relying on free ports	Defends a reform of the educational system and promotes for-profit education; defends the lowering of income and corporate taxes	Presided since 2020 by the owner of financial companies Michael Spencer (NEX Group, brokerage and clearing company)	Historically presided by the public relations executive Maurice Saatchi; supported by the construction tycoon Anthony Bamford (JC Bamford), the tobacco industry and the Spectator	Orders reports to numerous Conservative MPs and ministers, including Rishi Sunak and Dominic Raab

Name	Date of creation	Founders	Political goal	Position on climate change	Position on Brexit	Other political positions	Support from the financial sector	Other known support	Ties with political circles
Cobden Centre	2010	Conservative pro-Brexit MP Steve Baker, and libertarian entrepreneur Toby Baxendale	Defends the views of the Austrian school (Friedrich Hayek, Ludwig von Mises) in the British political debate	Considers that action to curb climate change should not weaken private property rights	Pro-hard Brexit and Eurosceptic from the start	Promotes the end of public intervention in the monetary system through technological solutions (cryptocurrencies)	Denounces the postcrisis European financial regulation	The think tank partly funds itself through its advisory branch dedicated to the financial sector, Cobden Partners	Several Cobden Centre executives participated in the Leave campaign and entered the government; founder Steve Baker became Parliamentary Under Secretary of State at DExEU in 2017
Global Warming Policy Foundation (GWPF)	2009	Conservative Thatcherian MP and former Chancellor of the Exchequer Lord Nigel Lawson	'Open-minded on the contested science of global warming, deeply concerned about the costs and other implications of many of the policies being currently advocated'	One of the main British think tanks that denies climate change	The GWPF does not have a position on Brexit, but its founder Lord Nigel Lawson was one of the leaders of Vote Leave Ltd		Sir Michael Hintze (CQS) and Neil Record (Record Currency Management), as for IEA	The GWPF refuses direct donations from the oil industry; donors come from the Conservative Party and industry (e.g. the paper mill industry, the Bristol Port Company)	No direct link with the Johnson government, but more direct ties with Conservative MPs and Lords (Peter Lilley, Matt Ridley, Nigel Vinson) and even some Labour MPs (Graham Stringer, Owen Paterson)

Name	Date of creation	Founders	Political goal	Position on climate change	Position on Brexit	Other political positions	Support from the financial sector	Other known support	Ties with political circles
Economists for Free Trade (formerly Economists for Brexit)	2015	Patrick Minford, professor of economics at the University of Cardiff, and a former advisor to Margaret Thatcher	Proving the economic advantages of Brexit	No position, but supports alignment of the UK with US environmental policy and regulations	Promotes a no-deal Brexit and the positive consequences of Brexit for the City			Co-directed by Edgar Miller, a US billionaire who made his fortune in shale oil; supported by David Ord, owner of the Bristol Port Company	Close to pro-Brexit MPs in the European Research Group; includes ministers Jacob Rees-Mogg, Owen Paterson and David Jones

rose from 6.5 per cent of all UK income in 1980 to 14 per cent in 2015.[29] These growing inequalities have been accompanied by a weakening of public services and the welfare state, following waves of privatisation and austerity reforms. The reform of social benefits adopted in 2012 imposed stricter conditions of eligibility for all social benefits, cut back the sums allocated and instituted a five-week waiting period before benefits are paid out, resulting in real hardship for many impoverished working-class households. The NHS has also suffered from both chronic underfunding and the health problems exacerbated by the withdrawal of the state from social matters. Even before the Covid-19 crisis, every year the NHS faced what the media called the 'winter crisis', when the waiting times for emergency health care soared. In 2017 patients waited over four hours for emergency hospital services in 25 per cent of cases. These extreme conditions have had consequences that were hardly imaginable a few decades ago. Whereas the life expectancy of the British people had been on the rise since the end of the nineteenth century, it has stagnated since 2011, and even fallen for some segments of the population, especially in the industrial wastelands of northern England, and for working-class women.[30] This was situation before the Covid-19 pandemic. Life expectancy has been falling for the country as a whole since 2020, but at higher rates among poor people.

After more than 30 years of neoliberalism, the libertarianism promoted by the Tufton Street literature seems to have reached the limits of what is socially acceptable under the British political regime of accumulation. The remaining spaces that capital could conquer are found in the last vestiges of the social heritage of the postwar period. First of these is the NHS, which most libertarian think tanks want to see privatised: the Adam Smith Institute, the Institute of Economic Affairs and the Initiative for Free Trade would like the NHS to be 'opened to international competition' in a trade deal with the United

States. In education, the IEA would replace state-operated schools with a so-called competitive educational market in which parents would receive 'vouchers' funded by the state and could choose to send their children to either public or private schools. Regarding minimum social and environmental norms, such as the 48-hour cap on weekly work hours, or the ban on chlorine-rinsed chickens, the Conservative minister Michael Gove, close to the Legatum Institute and the Initiative for Free Trade, has said they should be eliminated altogether.[31]

First-wave finance built its mode of accumulation on the large infrastructures of the country. Profits came mostly from the employees and consumers of large stock listed companies, recently privatised infrastructure, large banks, insurance companies and the pensions of these employees through pension funds. In short, the central core of the British economy. Second-wave finance extends financialisation to spaces from which it had been excluded. Brexit is nothing other than a step in this process. It opens up profit opportunities in areas of society that had previously been preserved from financialisation: small and medium-sized companies are targeted by private equity funds, the real estate market is upended by real estate investment funds, and many other parameters of social and economic are subject to speculation via derivative products created by hedge funds. Second-wave finance has also risen to institutional power through coalitions with sectors that are far from being progressive in social or environmental matters; the funding of the Brexit referendum and the association with Tufton Street think tanks reveals that second-wave finance is allied with fossil fuel and construction companies.

In this context, the contradiction between libertarian ideology and the restriction of public liberties is merely superficial. Even though the reduction of public liberties is not expressed as a core principle of libertarianism, it is one of its practical consequences. Under a regime that accepts inequalities and ignores the common good, and without any material mechanism to compensate for the impoverishment of significant segments of the population, the use of force is the only instrument left to regulate social life and enforce social order. Public liberties are sacrificed for the sake of the protection of the most essential of all liberties: the freedom to own and to accumulate.

Here our work echoes the research of US and European academics who since the mid-2010s have described the development of a new mode of social regulation based on repression and restriction of liberty.[32] Our approach diverges from some of this work: we call this rising mode of population management 'authoritarian' rather than 'totalitarian', 'fascist' or 'Bonapartist'. The notion of totalitarianism was popularised during the Cold War to portray communism and fascism as two strands of a similar mode of government, and thus drive a wedge into the united front of the right, the left and the far-left against European fascism that prevailed at the end of the Second World War.[33] As for fascism, this construct posits an almighty state opposed to any form of individuality outside of the state, as individuals are inherently prone to insubordination. The contemporary rising authoritarianism that we describe consists solely in the glorification of individual potentialities, ruling out any form of collective solidarity or state protection.[34] The authoritarianism we describe also diverges from Bonapartism, which as analysed by Marx provided theoretical grounds for the later analysis of fascism in the twentieth century. For Marx, Bonapartism is a form of bourgeois government that positions itself above social classes in order to govern and defend an order threatened by social movements.[35] In circumstances where the property of the economically dominant classes is threatened, they are obliged to tolerate the existence of a state apparatus they do not directly control, and that enforces social order with enormous and relatively autonomous military and police powers.[36] What we see today is not a transition to an autonomous state that would be mandated to resist the pressure of the rebellious working class. What we are witnessing is the merging of the dominant class and the state, a merger that threatens the economic, social and political existence of the dominated class. Marx described the surprise of the bourgeoisie when it realised that 'the weapons with which [it had] felled feudalism to the ground were now turned against the bourgeoisie itself', and that it had 'called into existence the men who were to wield those weapons – the proletarians'.[37] This description does not match the situation of second-wave finance, as Brexit is not the result of a massive mobilisation of the working class against the new financialisation. The current authoritarianism is not a reaction to a potential working-class insurgency but rather a project, a manifesto and a pre-emptive strike.

One has only to read the biographies of the main figures of the second-wave, pro-Brexit and libertarian financiers to perceive this hidden but strong alliance between economic deregulation and political authoritarianism. The careers of the pioneers of second-wave finance illustrate the relationship between these new financial sectors and authoritarianism. For instance, James Goldsmith, the heir of an old family of Frankfurt bankers, made his name in the City of the 1970s by launching the first 'corporate raids' – hostile takeovers of industrial companies. This activity would soon become the core business of private equity funds, one of the key sectors of second-wave finance. Goldsmith was not only one of the founders of the private equity business model, he was also a leading figure of the Eurosceptic front. Immediately following the Maastricht treaty, he founded the Referendum Party, the first British party to call for a referendum on Brexit. Goldsmith was elected to the European Parliament on a list featuring leaders of the French far-right. He also espoused strongly anti-trade union positions and practices. Up to the 1980s he supported the British paramilitary organisation GB75, coordinated by former SAS captain David Stirling, which aimed to infiltrate and disrupt British trade unions, and prepared an action plan for a military coup in case of a socialist takeover in Britain. Goldsmith remained a major donor to British Conservative movements until his death in 1998, and steadfastly supported the most authoritarian options to combat social movements.

In the current context, the proponents of second-wave finance seemingly no longer need democratic government. This contradicts the Marxist idea that liberal democracy is the form of government best suited to bourgeois domination. In Marxist thought, the bourgeoisie embraced liberal democracy because this new dominant class was threatened by rival elite groups in the exercise of power. In the early nineteenth century it was vital for the rising bourgeoisie to acquire legitimacy other than the legitimacy of family lines and heritage, to counter the interests of feudal and aristocratic classes who remained popular in some parts of the countryside. The bourgeoisie had to ward off a potential resurrection of the coalition between the landed aristocracy and the peasant classes that had prevailed in most European countries for almost a thousand years. In this context, the reinvention of democracy, based on the idea of a sovereign people, shored up the interests of the bourgeois revolution. Today the bourgeoisie is not threatened by any other rising class. In the absence of any monarchist or socialist threat, does the bourgeoisie still need democracy?

As in other European and Western democracies, we see the first signs of an authoritarian turn of the British regime with respect to civil and political liberties. On top of the attempt to illegally suspend the Parliament in 2019, successive antiterrorism bills passed between 2000 and 2015 have significantly strengthened the discretionary powers of the executive to control individuals. Now that the United Kingdom has left the European Union, pro-Brexit leaders from the Brexit Party and the Conservative Party such as Nigel Farage and Jacob Rees-Mogg also seek to drop out of the European Court of Human Rights.[38] While moderate in comparison to the repression of the miners' strikes under Margaret Thatcher and the treatment of the 'yellow vests' in France, the British executive is growing tougher on social movements. This is especially true for environmental movements: the actions and demonstrations of Extinction Rebellion in London in October 2019, for instance, were strongly repressed. Using public order legislation introduced by the Thatcher government in 1986, the Metropolitan Police Service banned all demonstrations by the environmental group for the whole month. In two weeks more than 1,600 environmentalist militants were arrested, according to police reports. This repression was encouraged by the intellectuals of the coming political regime of accumulation. The Institute of Economic Affairs wrote that the Extinction Rebellion demonstrations raised 'difficult [questions] for liberals and libertarians', but that as the group 'deliberately broke the law to cause economic damage' the think tank supported the ban on their demonstrations. It also encouraged the police to 'act firmly' to put an end to the actions of a group that it deemed 'extremist', going as far as to assert that some of Extinction Rebellion's activities, such as the use of drones to disturb London's Heathrow airport and its contested extension project, 'had flirted with dangerous terrorist offences'.[39]

The present-day authoritarian tendency is not a response to a pre-existing popular threat, nor is it solely an expression of the crisis of free-market capitalism. Karl Polanyi analysed the fascist movements of the 1930s as the consequence of the crisis of free-market capitalism and its grounding ideology.[40] Fascism appears in a period of withdrawal of states into autarchy, during which 'fascist mass movements claim to work towards the regeneration of an "imaginary community" considered to be organic (nation, "race", civilisation)'.[41] This representation assumes that the liberal democratic form of government remains the norm in a capitalist regime, and that authoritarianism is a deviant form of government, sometimes chosen for lack of a better alternative, in the emergency of an institutional or social crisis. But in today's situation, the crisis of liberal democracy did not precede the preference given to authoritarianism by the new dominating class. On the contrary, it is the choice of authoritarianism by the new dominating class that has triggered the crisis of liberal democracy.

The libertarian-authoritarian political regime of accumulation is not a response to actual social disorders; rather, it is the instrument that new accumulators have taken up to protect themselves from future threats. To understand this, we need to take seriously what the neoliberal regime has done to society.[42] To perpetuate itself, capitalism has to reconcile interests within the dominant classes, at least provisionally, and obtain from the working class a minimum level of consent to the existing regime. By a minimum level of consent, we mean that even if discontent provokes social unrest this unrest should not disturb the process of accumulation itself. Obtaining the minimal consent of the working class has traditionally been the job of what Pierre Bourdieu called the 'left hand of the state' (broadly speaking, the welfare state).[43] The task is to create a 'historical bloc' able to integrate social classes with diverging interests in a common society.[44] But neoliberal reforms have dismantled the welfare state and the left hand of the state is increasingly empty; Keynesian ideas have disappeared from governmental institutions and the main mechanisms of social integration have broken down. The dominated classes have not, for now, been converted to socialist ideas in any significant way, but they are saturated with discontent to the extent that additional waves of deregulation could lead to outbursts of popular anger. Authoritarian libertarianism protects the hard-won gains made by accumulators during the period of European neoliberalism to suppress the expression of discontent, and paves the way for further expansion of their 'right' to accumulate.

Brexit was a first stone thrown at the previous political regime of accumulation by the new financial actors, whose political aims could take hold on a global scale. The electoral victories of Viktor Orbán in Hungary in 2010, Andrzej Duda in Poland in 2015, Donald Trump in the United States in 2016 and Jair Bolsonaro in Brazil in 2018 are signs of the advent of a new moment for capitalism. The links between pro-Brexit and pro-Trump forces are strong; the think tanks that elaborate their ideology are grouped within the Atlas Foundation and their money often comes from the same sources. The most active sectors of second-wave finance, i.e. hedge funds and private equity funds, also finance a new brand of politicians in the United States and Brazil, politicians who defend alternative political projects. Although they have suffered from the hostility of neoliberal institutions and their corporate backers, these new political actors have capitalised on the support of second-wave finance to grow and attain the top echelons of power.

The oft-heralded end of European neoliberalism as a dominant political regime of accumulation in Western countries is not the consequence of the manipulation of credulous voters, the xenophobic discourse of demagogues, new communication networks and the propagation of fake news that they make possible, or any other purely ideological process. It is not a matter of propaganda or influence exerted on the malleable minds of disoriented citizens. It is the project of a recent faction of the financial community in competition with older financial sectors. Driven by its own mode of capital accumulation, this new financial faction is determined to consolidate and even expand its enrichment opportunities, challenging the financial hegemony of first-wave financial actors. The new political regime anticipates the growing social tensions generated by the expansion of financial accumulation. But why has this regime emerged so suddenly at one time and in such different quarters of the globe? What is the explanation for the fact that in places very far from each other – Eastern European countries, the United States, Brazil and the United Kingdom – the most aggressive and profitable subsectors of finance have opted for authoritarian libertarianism?

A political regime of accumulation tailored to the new climate regime

As Bruno Latour has recently written, 'one cannot understand anything about political positions in the last five decades if one does not give a central place to the issue of climate'.[45] The political regime of accumulation that we describe takes place in a specific geohistorical context. This context, what Latour calls the 'new climate regime', pertains to the circumstances that threaten the survival of a growing portion of humanity, including (and this is new) in so-called Global North countries. This fact cannot be ignored, and certainly not at the level of information, financial might and economic power that characterises the new financial actors, who increasingly invest in the financialisation of environmental action. The reality of climate change occupies a central place in the elaboration of the political regime of accumulation that aims to maximise the well-being and the accumulation possibilities for its proponents in the next decades.

This emergent political regime is linked in many ways to what, barring a momentous historical awakening, we can already characterise as a looming environmental disaster. The coming disaster represents an opportunity for second-wave finance to extend its activity to ecosystems and the environment, with new prospects for accumulation. For these operators, 'the ecological crisis [could become] a fantastic economic opportunity'.[46] That is, unless a regional or international institution suddenly decides to curb financial speculation on the preservation of living beings and ecosystems. The organised climate change denial movements of the 2000s were a key vector in the effort to prevent any attempt to regulate the financial exploitation of the environment. This does not mean that climate change deniers do not believe in the science of the IPCC experts; it means only that they believe preventing climate change would come at an exorbitant cost to themselves. Climate change denial is less a matter of personal faith regarding climate change and the resultant ecosystem collapse than of the conviction that there are no political and economic solutions acceptable to those who benefit the most from the current accumulation system. It is a tactical choice that justifies refusing the institutional changes that could, perhaps, lessen the impact of the disaster. As Naomi Klein has written, 'we are stuck because the actions that would give us the best chance of averting catastrophe – and would benefit the vast majority – are extremely threatening to an elite minority that has a stranglehold over our economy'.[47]

It is telling that climate change denial is widespread in the pro-Brexit campaign. Several of its leaders, including Lord Nigel Lawson and Jacob Rees-Mogg, have questioned the anthropogenic origin of the climate change observed today. Lawson, a prominent British climate denier, founded the Global Warming Policy Foundation in 2009. This foundation is in infringement of the rules of the UK Charity Commission because of its 'political rather than educational' positions on climate change. It also shares many donors with the Vote Leave campaign. At the time of this writing Jacob Rees-Mogg is a minister in Boris Johnson's government, a vocal supporter of Brexit and a hedge fund manager. In 2013 he denounced the abandonment of coal energy by the Conservative government of the time. In 2014 he declared that he would prefer that the United Kingdom 'adapt' to climate change rather than 'going back to living in the stone-age by reducing people's use of energy'.[48]

Those who aim to extend the financialisation process to the environment rely on a key idea: each natural element should be attributed an economic value, a price that would correspond to the value of its ecosystem services, that is to say the value it provides to humans, to whom it can be sold – at least to those who can pay. In 2007 Ricardo Bayon cofounded EKO Asset Management Partners, an investment fund specialised in natural assets. In the early 2000s, he set up a website and information platform called Ekosystem Marketplace, that operates in emerging environmental markets. He advocates for carbon emission markets and the generalisation of biobanks, which allow companies to offer financial compensation to offset the destruction of precious ecosystems. He is currently a member of the board of the investment fund Encourage Capital, where he manages the team in charge of water-related transactions. He openly explains that in the previous historical period, capital and labour were scarce and, consequently, expensive commodities, but that in the coming period the most lucrative investments will come from the rarefaction of the services that natural ecosystems provide.[49]

The environmental crisis is here exploited as a growth driver for second-wave finance, fostering the development of what is known as 'impact investment funds'. This term designates transactions involving environmental and social assets that are executed, guaranteed or financed by such funds (environmental impact investment and social impact investment). This category of investment has grown considerably since the first impact investment fund, Bridges Ventures, was set up in the UK by the former private equity fund manager Sir Ronald Cohen. Second-wave financiers, including Sir Ronald, have actively supported the emergence of the sector through numerous working groups on social impact investment successively convened by the governments of Tony Blair, Gordon Brown and David Cameron.[50] This new financial sector has even chosen the United Kingdom as its main diplomatic instrument. In 2013, when the UK was organising the G8 summit, Cameron decided to dedicate one of the task forces of the event to the promotion of impact investment. Each G8 country was to send a delegation to this task force, chaired by none other than Sir Ronald Cohen, to reflect on ways to foster the development of social and environmental finance in their respective national financial sectors. Given this boost, the growth of impact investment funds is hardly surprising: nonexistent in the UK in the early 2000s, these funds raised £8.9 billion in 2007 and almost £16 billion in 2017.[51] These new actors are attracted by the prospect of reforming British social and environmental policies, especially if these reforms are grounded on principles of deregulation and financialisation.

Second-wave finance adopts the precepts of the New Resource Economy developed by Harold Desmetz and Armen Alchian, which puts private property rights at the heart of environmental preservation. Inspired by the Chicago school and the work of Ronald Coase and Garrett Hardin (who in 1968 published his famous *Science* article on the 'Tragedy of the Commons'), second-wave finance has integrated the idea that collective management of a common environmental good would be incompatible with its sustainable use. It also adopts the view of free-market environmentalism popularised by Robert Smith in 1979. This approach posits that no one has an interest in taking individual action to preserve resources that are owned in common. Consequently, to protect environmental resources it is best to fully privatise them so that each portion of the natural world has an owner (and keeper). In this perspective, the regional and international institutions that aim to deploy stringent mechanisms to collectively address the depletion of environmental resources are an obstacle, as they stand in the way of second-wave finance and its goal of maximising financial accumulation derived from the environmental crisis. These operators contend that natural resources would be more efficiently regulated by the market than by governments.

Second-wave finance has attained political hegemony at a time when capitalist logic is expanding towards new spaces beyond its present boundaries. This includes environmental resources. As David Harvey describes it, following the analyses of Rosa Luxemburg, 'capitalism must perpetually have something "outside of itself" in order to stabilize'.[52] He refutes the Marxist thesis that the violent primitive accumulation of the past constituted the necessary and revolutionary basis for contemporary accumulation, but that it was now over and had left the floor to 'expanded reproduction', a process of accumulation that takes place via peaceful contractual relationships between capitalists and workers. His theory is that to maintain itself as the dominant mode of accumulation, capitalism has to constantly transform new things into commodities by building relationships (and often conflicts) with noncapitalist spaces of social life. These things can be public services, territories or living beings, and they are appropriated through what Harvey calls 'dispossession'. 'The general thrust of any capitalistic logic of power is not that territories should be held back from capitalist development, but that they should be continuously opened up.'[53] For a time, dispossession occurred in the form of imperial conquest, privatisation and financialisation. It now occurs as the commodification of scarce environmental resources. The watchword of the actors supporting this new wave of appropriation can be summarised as follows: let us dispossess freely, without interference from either the European Union or national states, as we move to appropriate ecosystems and scarce environmental resources.

Our last observation is that this new political regime of accumulation does not aim for the sustainable reproduction of the dominant classes. It does not embody its own justification as do other forms of domination, which are posited variously on inherited wealth and privilege, academic merit, existential asceticism, innate charisma, taste for risk, or business acumen. It does not make any pretence of contributing to the common good or social progress. It does not even lay the grounds for the founding of secular dynasties of bold financiers. It does not create mythological figures dedicated to enlightening the masses. In other words, it is not built to last. It does not offer horizontal solidarity with the rest of the population to ensure minimal conditions of existence for people, nor does it celebrate vertical solidarity with ancestors and progeny, as it does not seek to legitimate and perpetuate domination. It is as if the dominant class 'had been so convinced that there would be no future life for anyone that they decided to get rid as quickly as possible of all the burdens of solidarity', whether material or symbolic.[54]

The conflict that we are witnessing is an opposition between what Bruno Latour calls 'modern' and 'out-of-this-world' individuals (in French *hors sol*). 'Modern' financiers are deeply convinced (in good faith or simply to advance their own interests) that science and technology will provide us with the means to conjure away our bad climate destiny, stimulated by a capitalism that is deemed to be the only available instrument for the optimal allocation of capital. 'Out-of-this-world' financiers do not delude themselves that capitalism can help us out of the difficult climatic situation in which it has put us: they are simply determined to accumulate as much capital as they can and enjoy it while it is still possible to do so, or to be well placed when the tension surrounding access to the last remaining vital resources reaches breaking point. Out-of-this-world financiers have no doubt that capitalism does not mean progress, in the sense of an improvement in the conditions of collective social life. Echoing an (implicit) elitist survivalist ideology or a nihilistic hedonist one, they simply want to empty the shop before it closes. In other words, they seek the absolute right to accumulate all the goods, territories and capital that are still extant in a world under the threat of extinction. As Latour puts it: 'For the first time, we observe a large-scale movement that does not seriously pretend to face geopolitical realities, but rather tries to put itself explicitly outside of all worldly constraints, literally offshore, like a tax haven.'[55] The libertarian-authoritarian regime of accumulation that we have described is to be understood in the context of a new climate regime; a regime that takes environmental collapse into account, into its accounts, by making the maxim 'every man for himself' into a universal doctrine and institutionalising the secessionist aims of a part of the dominant class to the detriment of the rest of humanity.

Epilogue:
The Drumbeat of War

Second-wave finance, a geopolitical force

The British case is not an isolated one. Other countries are on the brink of shifting towards a libertarian-authoritarian accumulation regime. Even for those in which the neoliberal regime still dominates, the pressure of actors supporting the new regime is considerable and growing. In this context, three types of national configuration are emerging.

The first configuration is found in several countries where second-wave financial actors have built up coalitions strong enough to tip the power balance in their favour in the political arena.[1] These coalitions embed second-wave finance at the heart of the new accumulation regime. This is the case in the United Kingdom and the United States, although the battle continues between economic actors who support the neoliberal regime and the proponents of a libertarian-authoritarian regime. In both countries the shift has been due to internal forces, thanks to a reconfiguration of the balance of power between economic sectors and to its consequences for political institutions. These transitions have been supported by the founders of second-wave financial organisations, which are at the core of the nascent coalitions that have reset the political balance and secured hegemonic power in these countries. This shift in power has given a pulpit to new intellectual voices and libertarian ideologues, and fostered new institutions and the election of representatives who defend the interests of second-wave finance. It has also created new divisions in the business community, as all other economic sectors, and not only finance, are obliged to position themselves in the conflict between the defenders of the neoliberal regime and the promoters of the libertarian-authoritarian regime. If we look closely, it is likely that we will find in Silicon Valley a similar split to the one observed in the UK and US financial sectors – between very visible neoliberal actors and the more discreet promoters of a libertarian-authoritarian break with the existing state of affairs. Situations similar to those observed in the UK and the US can be seen elsewhere in the world, and not only in so-called 'developed' countries. Brazil, for instance, has undergone what is a very far-ranging financialisation process for an emerging country. In 2017, the financial sector accounted for 7.6 per cent of Brazil's GDP, a proportion similar to the UK, and São Paulo was the main financial centre for funding directed to South America. In 2014, 90 per cent of the trade in financial derivatives in the continent was handled in São Paulo, and the city was home to many hedge funds.[2] In this context, the election of Jair Bolsonaro can be interpreted as the most recent step up in the ascension of a particularly antisocial and anti-ecological coalition, comprising both agricultural interests favourable to deforestation in the Amazon and increasingly powerful South American fund managers.

The second configuration is seen in countries that have welcomed a developed financial sector and many second-wave financial actors but do not appear to be engaged in a shift in their regime of accumulation. A notable example is Ireland, where the massive financial sector and numerous hedge funds seem to coexist peacefully with neoliberal institutions. This is also the case in France, the Netherlands and Italy. These countries are characterised by well-ensconced financial sectors. A host of second-wave financial actors have emerged in the last decades in these countries, but accumulation regimes have not been significantly reorganised. In these countries the neoliberal accumulation regime is under pressure from the inside, but the advocates of the new libertarian-authoritarian regime have obtained only modest changes and not a radical shift. A number of factors shape this configuration. The financial sectors of these countries are still less powerful than the financial sectors of the countries of the first configuration – the French and Italian economies are less financialised than in the UK. Most importantly, second-wave financial actors do not yet have a hegemonic position in the financial sector. Hedge funds and private equity funds do not have the clout in, say, the Dutch financial sector that they have in Britain. Furthermore, the political intentions of the new financiers collide head-on with the fundamental grounding of these countries in supranational institutions. France, the Netherlands and Italy belong to the EU, dominated by Germany, a country with a small financial sector in which second-wave finance is almost nonexistent.

The third configuration is found in countries that are not engaged in the development of second-wave finance but which act in synergy with the emerging libertarian-authoritarian accumulation regime. It would be nonsense to attribute the recent political transformations in Poland and Hungary to the rise in power of second-wave finance. These two countries have indeed shifted towards authoritarian nationalism, but their governments cannot rely on a financial force that is practically nonexistent in their countries. However, these governments do have objective affinities with the libertarian-authoritarian regime, which puts pressure on the neoliberal regime. In Poland the right-wing authoritarian government is dependent on the sectors that export coal and cheap labour. Poland naturally has reasons to support social and environmental deregulation at the international level as desired by the most financialised countries.

As we would expect, the transformation of the accumulation regimes of the US, the UK and Brazil (ranking first, sixth and ninth in the global economy) has had major geopolitical consequences. Libertarian-authoritarianism is not an isolationist regime; it joins up and articulates the interests of the dominant classes of countries in the avant-garde of capitalism (and the interests of their exuberant financial fortunes) with those of the dominant classes of countries that had been less influential in the longstanding neoliberal international order. The emergence of the libertarian-authoritarian regime relies on international coalitions that include countries governed by other regimes. Second-wave financiers do not need to dominate the economies of all countries in order to defend their interests at the international level. The states that have been converted to the libertarian-authoritarian accumulation regime can agree deals with states that are dominated by other economic forces but which share their desire to dismantle the minimal international, social and environmental regulations that persist under the neoliberal regime. What is at stake in Europe right now is not only the more or less rapid ascension of a new financial force but also the emergence of potential allies for the advocates of the new regime of accumulation, including in countries with small financial sectors.

The everyday consequences of the libertarian-authoritarian accumulation regime

The spread of the libertarian-authoritarian regime is a crucial phenomenon, as it entails concrete consequences for people. It deepens the financialisation of societies, widening the gap between rich and poor. Inequalities of income and wealth are rising, and approaching the level of the early twentieth century. This regime transforms many aspects of the daily life of individuals into sources of profit, including social and environmental policies that had escaped financialisation until now. It results in widespread and diverse changes: public funding for education is replaced by private student debt, charities and social enterprises in the tertiary sector are transformed into centres of financial profit, and natural and agricultural spaces become tradeable commodities.

This shift also has huge environmental consequences. Through the subsidies and tax cuts that it demands, and obtains, the financial sector is placing a heavy burden on public finances. Access to common goods is increasingly in question. Between 2014 and 2017 the 100,000 inhabitants of the city of Flint, near Detroit, Michigan, were exposed to lead in their drinking water supply as a result of the budgetary crisis that affected their city. French localities have been hit by similar water supply crises, also linked to budgetary restrictions. These places are mostly in French overseas territories and in poor neighbourhoods. The NGO Coalition Eau estimates that 1 million people in France do not have adequate access to water. More broadly, the reluctance of the US and Brazilian governments to follow through on the objectives of the Paris agreements on climate change, and the decision of the UK government not to follow the environmental directives of the EU, have resulted in wildfires in California and Brazil and landslides in England. Climate disturbance triggers extreme weather events around the globe, for which libertarian-authoritarian regimes reject any form of collective reparation.

The Covid-19 crisis has also shown how a shift in accumulation regimes can have far-reaching consequences in unexpected areas of social life. In the UK, the intellectuals of the new regime of accumulation were already present in the political debate before the Brexit referendum, solicited by some members of the Conservative Party and by second-wave financiers. As early as the 2010s, behavioural economists and libertarian think tanks had weighed in on British public health doctrine. They were already defending public health policies based exclusively on individual responsibility and the privatisation of health care, and they were critical of any centralised policy to manage pandemics. When Covid-19 gripped Europe in the early months of 2020, Boris Johnson's government leaned heavily on talking points from these intellectuals, going so far as to envision a 'herd immunity' approach to the pandemic.[3] Simultaneously, these states engaged in trade wars with their neighbours and former partners to appropriate the material resources needed to fight the virus. Donald Trump's administration sought to buy out CureVac, a German pharmaceutical company involved in promising vaccine research, to ensure US citizens exclusive access to the first deliveries of doses. Similarly, Boris Johnson's government decided to proceed with purely national calls for tenders and not to participate in the European call for artificial respirators and protective equipment, which was designed precisely to avoid predatory competition between European countries.

The spread of conflicts to the North

By changing the global balance of power, the new libertarian-authoritarian accumulation regime also contributes to a new geopolitical situation. The international neoliberal order sustained a radical global divide. On one side were the so-called 'North' countries, linked by multiple agreements: military commitments under the NATO alliance, regional economic treaties, political agreements made through the European Union and the G7 group. On the other side lay the so-called 'South' countries, essentially the playground of the capitalist forces of rich countries that dragged these (poor) countries into conflicts of all sorts: endless trade conflicts with relentless social and fiscal dumping, and military conflicts supported by the North to take control of their resources, markets and workforce. The emerging international order would appear to put an end to this decades-old divide, but it does not do so by ending conflicts in the South. Instead it seems to have rescinded the tacit nonaggression pact between Northern states.

In their quest for new profit opportunities the promoters of the new accumulation regime no longer fear conflicts between 'developed' countries. Fiscal competition between states has increased in the wake of the Trump administration's decision to lower the corporate tax rate from 35 per cent to 21 per cent in 2017 (a decision that has not been reversed by the Biden administration). Trade competition has also grown stronger. The order established by the World Trade Organization and successive GATT agreements has now collapsed, following the United States' decision not to renew its judges in the WTO dispute settlement body. The WTO aimed to contain trade tensions in the neoliberal structure to avoid a return to the trade wars of the 1930s – the de facto dismantling of WTO mechanisms will likely encourage policies that could ignite trade wars again. This vacuum allows emerging libertarian-authoritarian regimes to pressure their trading partners to serve the interests they represent. It was from this perspective that, following Brexit, the British government declared its intention to free itself from EU social and environmental norms in order to sign trade deals with the rest of the world and open up new markets for UK products and capital.

Beyond trade conflicts, it cannot be ignored that the representatives of the new accumulation regime have also pivoted away from the institutions and instruments created to maintain peace in the North (and often war in the South). These include NATO, the traditionally interventionist foreign policy of the US, the EU edifice, multilateral international institutions (the UN, the G7 and the G20 groups), and arms control treaties inherited from the Cold War period. The cost of peace among Northern countries may become too high for these governments, in the first place for the federal government of the United States, in a world where the capitalist actors it represents now seem able to survive in times of catastrophic events such as wars and even profit from them. Second-wave financial actors are far from playing the role of 'peace brokers' that Karl Polanyi attributed to high finance in the late nineteenth century. Unlike their distant ancestors, second-wave financiers do not seem to be ready to pay the cost of collective policing to preserve the world order.

This does not mean that the situation in the South is likely to improve in the near future. The British and US governments have clearly voiced their intention to redefine their foreign policy, to align it more closely with the interests of their dominant national sectors, and without bothering to attach it to objectives of poverty reduction. Some parts of their foreign policy are being put under the direct control of the financial sector, as international development aid is progressively replaced by 'impact investments' managed jointly with large private investment funds in the respective countries. These governments do not intend to guarantee peace in the South any more than they had previously. What is new is that they do not aim to guarantee peace in the North any longer either. These trends give us a foretaste of the future when the North will face issues that have up to now been confined to the global South — lack of water and other essential resources (food, medicines), unchecked pollution that threatens human habitat, extreme poverty, and the irruption of military conflicts on a scale unknown under the neoliberal world order.

Know your enemy

Brexit has highlighted the struggle between the mainstays of the declining European neoliberal regime of accumulation and the proponents of the new regime under construction. This new regime is no cause for rejoicing: it opens up new perspectives of profit accumulation via a political orientation that combines libertarianism, authoritarianism and climate change denial.

Are leftist forces doomed as a consequence to give their support to a quite unlikely coalition of blue-collar workers and neoliberal first-wave financiers to protect the European treaties? No. It is an illusion to believe that the institutions of European neoliberalism and their supporters could be potential allies for social movements, simply in the hope that they would constitute a temporary obstacle to the political project of a new wave of financial actors. The recent history of Brexit shows how quickly the losing fractions of the business community can accept their defeat and reposition themselves advantageously in the new political regime of accumulation. If a similar shift were to occur in continental Europe, the dominant sectors of the neoliberal regime – large banks, insurance companies, industrial corporations – would promptly negotiate the terms of their allegiance to the new regime.

Neoliberalism offers no solid bulwark against the conflicts triggered by second-wave finance, and there is no going back to the previous status quo. Neither the neoliberal regime nor its Fordist predecessor addresses the challenges posed by the emergence of libertarian-authoritarian powers, at a time of accelerating climate change, rising social inequality and increasing global tensions. There is no good reason to regret the decline of the neoliberal accumulation regime. Rather, it is time to recognise the new face of our adversaries. They have just recently gone through a mutation on the European and American continents. They now threaten the minimum level of social harmony, peace and environmental resources required by free societies. At the same time, pockets of resistance are taking hold, new social movements are developing and new organisations are being created. The future of our daily lives and material environments depends on the outcome of these new struggles.

Notes

Preface

1. See Stephanie Kirchgaessner, 'Billionaires Backed Republicans Who Sought to Reverse US Election Results', *Guardian*, 15 January 2021.

2. See for instance the role of the libertarian MP Steve Baker, who supported Boris Johnson's hard line on Brexit before opposing him in an extremely confrontational way. Ben Wright, 'Steve Baker MP: I'm Sick of the Cabinet Sitting There Fat, Dumb and Happy', *Daily Telegraph*, 22 April 2022.

3. See Benjamin Braun, 'Asset Management Capitalism as a Corporate Governance Regime', in Jacob S. Hacker, Alexander Hertel-Fernandez, Paul Pierson and Kathleen Thelen (eds.), *American Political Economy: Politics, Markets, Power*, New York, Cambridge University Press, 2021, pp. 270–94; Kean Birch and Fabian Muniesa, *Assetization: Turning Things into Assets in Technoscientific Capitalism*, Boston, MIT Press, 2020; and Daniela Gabor, 'The Wall Street Consensus in Pandemic Times: What Does It Mean for Climate-aligned Development?', *Canadian Journal of Development Studies/Revue canadienne d'études du développement*, 42(1–2), 2021, pp. 238–51.

4. William Davies and Nicholas Gane have published a special issue of *Theory, Culture, and Society* on 'post-neoliberalism'. See their 'Post-Neoliberalism? An Introduction', *Theory, Culture, and Society*, 38(6), 2021, pp. 3–28, and in the same issue: Melinda Cooper, 'The Alt-Right: Neoliberalism, Libertarianism, and the Fascist Temptation' (pp. 29–50); Quinn Slobodian, 'The Backlash Against Globalization From Above: Elite Origins of the Crisis of the New Constitutionalism' (pp. 51–69). Glenn Morgan and Christian Lyhne Ibsen have also published a special issue of *Politics*

& Society on quiet politics in an era of noisy politics. See their 'Quiet Politics and Business Power: New Perspectives in an Era of Noisy Politics', *Politics & Society*, 49(1), 2021, pp. 3–16, and in the same issue: André Mach, Thomas David, Stéphanie Ginalski and Felix Bühlmann, 'From Quiet to Noisy Politics: Transformations of Swiss Business Elites' Power' (pp. 17–41); Pepper D. Culpepper, 'Quiet Politics in Tumultuous Times: Business Populism, and Democracy' (pp. 133–43).

Introduction

1. Thais Bilenky, 'Não temos receio algun de um governo Bolsonaro, afirma presidente da CNI', *Folha de S. Paulo*, 19 July 2018.

2. Arnaud Leparmentier, 'Si le Brexit nous était conté', *Le Monde*, 24 June 2016.

3. On this issue, see the work of Paul Pierson, who argues that we are witnessing the 'merging of plutocracy and populism', and of Ronald Inglehart and Pippa Norris, who directly refer to the social geography of the vote: Paul Pierson, 'American Hybrid: Donald Trump and the Strange Merger of Populism and Plutocracy', *British Journal of Sociology*, 68(1), 2017, pp. 105–9; Ronald Inglehart and Pippa Norris, 'Trump and the Populist Authoritarian Parties: The Silent Revolution in Reverse', *Perspectives on Politics*, 5(2), 2017, pp. 443–54. Likewise, Jonathan Hopkin analyses the Leave vote as a reaction to neoliberal policies, stemming from the desire to 're-embed' the economy within the social and political realms: Jonathan Hopkin, 'When Polanyi Met Farage: Market Fundamentalism, Economic Nationalism, and Britain's Exit from the European Union', *British Journal of Politics and International Relations*, 19(3), 2017, pp. 465–78.

4. William Davies, 'The Age of Post-Truth Politics', *New York Times*, 24 August 2016.

5. See Jipson John and Jitheesh P. M., 'The Neoliberal Project Is Alive But Has Lost Its Legitimacy: David Harvey', *The Wire*, 9 February 2019, and David Harvey's interview with Evgeny Morozov, 'David Harvey and Evgeny Morozov on Trump,

Neoliberalism, Infrastructure and "the Sharing Economy"', Verso blog, 14 November 2016: https://www.versobooks.com/blogs/3134-video-david-harvey-and-evgeny-morozov-on-trump-neoliberalism-infrastructure-and-the-sharing-economy.

6. See William Davies and Nicholas Gane, 'Post-neoliberalism? An Introduction', *Theory, Culture & Society*, 38(6), 2021, pp. 3–28.

7. See Quinn Slobodian, 'The Backlash Against Neoliberal Globalization from Above: Elite Origins of the Crisis of the New Constitutionalism', *Theory, Culture, Society*, 38(6), 2021, pp. 51–69.

8. See McKenzie Wark, *Capital Is Dead: Is This Something Worse?*, London, Verso, 2019.

9. This book builds on recent discussions in social sciences related to the rise of authoritarianism; see especially Wendy Brown, *In the Ruins of Neoliberalism: The Rise of Antidemocratic Politics in the West*, New York, Columbia University Press, 2019; and Grégoire Chamayou, *The Ungovernable Society: A Genealogy of Authoritarian Liberalism*, London, Polity, 2021. Many of these works deal with authoritarianism by stressing the political causes of the restriction of civil rights. By contrast, in this book, we point out how economic interests support the development of authoritarian political regimes.

10. The distinction between first- and second-wave finance, and the distinction between financial subsectors that it entails, are discussed in greater length in Chapter 1.

11. Several empirical works have investigated the effects of political funding on the vote. In their study of voting in France, Julia Cagé and Yasmine Bekkouche underline the massive effect of campaign spending on electoral outcomes. They estimate that for the 1993–2014 period, the average cost of a vote was €8 for French legislative elections, and €32 for French local elections. See Julia Cagé and Yasmine Bekkouche, 'The Price of a Vote: Evidence from France, 1993–2014', *CEPR Discussion Paper*, DP12614, 2018; and more recently: Yasmine Bekkouche, Julia Cagé and Edgard Dewitte, 'The Heterogeneous Price of a Vote: Evidence from Multiparty Systems, 1993–2017', *Journal of Public Economics*, 206, 2022. These findings enable Julia Cagé to compare national

models for the regulation of campaign spending and to show their effect on the vote and the orientation of democratic decisions. See Julia Cagé, *Le Prix de la démocratie*, Paris, Fayard, 2018.

12. This book is not the first piece of scholarship to take this approach to the Brexit referendum. In October 2016, Transparency International published a report on the funding of the campaign that showed the support of some financial sectors for the Leave vote. But the report did not offer any explanation for this support and it dealt with only a portion of campaign donations, not the full range as we have attempted to do. See Transparency International, *Take Back Control: How Big Money Undermines Trust in Politics*, London, Transparency International UK, 2016.

13. In this book, we rely on three sets of empirical material: the Electoral Commission database that lists all the donations to the campaigning groups in the Brexit referendum from 1 April to 31 October 2016; a corpus of 150 articles from the specialised (financial) and general newspapers reporting the positions of British and European financial actors on Brexit; and biographical information on the financial actors engaged in the Brexit campaign, and later in the negotiation of the Brexit agreement with the European Union.

1   The Big Money Behind Brexit

1. Cécile Ducourtieux, Raphaëlle Bacqué and Philippe Bernard, 'La saga du Brexit, saison 1: la brouille', *Le Monde*, 30 March 2019.
2. 'EU Backs Juncker to Head Commission in Blow to UK', BBC News, 27 June 2014.
3. Cécile Ducourtieux, Raphaëlle Bacqué and Philippe Bernard, 'La saga du Brexit, saison 1: la brouille', *Le Monde*, 30 March 2019.
4. See the work of François-Xavier Dudouet and Eric Grémont, 'Les grands patrons et l'Etat en France, 1981–2007', *Sociétés contemporaines*, 4(68), 2007, pp. 105–31; Carlos Ramirez, 'Du commissariat aux comptes à l'audit. Les Big 4 et la profession comptable depuis 1970', *Actes de la recherche en sciences sociales*, 146–7, 2003, pp. 62–79; François Denord, Paul Lagneau-Ymonet and Sylvain Thine, 'Le champ du pouvoir en France', *Actes de la recherche en*

sciences sociales, 190, 2011, pp. 24–57; François Denord and Paul Lagneau-Ymonet, *Le Concert des puissants*, Paris, Raisons d'agir, 2016.

5. See Jacob S. Hacker and Paul Pierson, *Winner-Take-All Politics: How Washington Made the Rich Richer and Turned its Back on the Middle Class*, New York, Simon & Schuster, 2010; and Sylvain Laurens, *Lobbyists and Bureaucrats in Brussels: Capitalism's Brokers*, Abingdon, Routledge, 2018.

6. Cornelia Woll shows that the ability of dominant groups to influence the government to their own advantage is not necessarily tied to the strength of collective organisations and lobbying groups, but to a more *structural* power that these dominant groups are able to exert on the state: Cornelia Woll, 'Politics in the Interest of Capital: A Not-So-Organized Combat', *Politics and Society*, 44(3), 2016, pp. 373–91.

7. Ralph Miliband, *L'Etat dans la société capitaliste. Analyse du système du pouvoir occidental*, translated by Christos Passadéos, Paris, Maspero, 1979, p. 57.

8. See Nicos Poulantzas, *State, Power, Socialism*, London, Verso, 2013 [1978].

9. See Rowena Mason, 'UK Trade Union Leaders Call on 6 Million Members to Vote Remain', *Guardian*, 6 June 2016.

10. 'The EU: Should Britain Be In or Out?', *Observer*, 18 January 2014.

11. The European financial passport gives any company that has been granted certification for banking and/or financial activity by the national regulatory agency of its country of origin the right to exercise this activity in all other countries of the European Economic Area (EEA), which includes Iceland, Liechtenstein and Norway in addition to the member states of the European Union. This 'passporting' authorises companies to sell banking and financial services to the whole EEA from a single place. This European rule was one of the key components of the pre-eminence of London as a financial centre, as the City played the role of a gateway to the European continent for foreign companies, especially US corporations.

12. A clearing house is an entity that manages the risk of trade settlement to facilitate financial trades. Clearing houses ensure risk-free delivery of the payments, securities and derivatives that investors exchange on markets.

13. See Raphaël Legendre, 'Il n'est pas inconcevable que la Grande-Bretagne reste dans l'Europe', *L'Opinion*, 10 July 2016.

14. See Vincent Gayon and Benjamin Lemoine, 'Maintenir l'ordre économique. Politiques de désencastrement et de réencastrement de l'économie', *Politix*, 105, 2014, pp. 7–35.

15. For each donation, we identified the sector or subsector in which the donating company or individual operates. This information forms the basis for a new variable: the 'economic sector' of origin for each donation.

16. Karl Marx, *The Eighteenth Brumaire of Louis Bonaparte*, Moscow, Progress Publishers, 1937 [1852], chapter 3.

17. Although Arron Banks's holdings are diversified and opaque, making their analysis difficult, we have decided to classify him as a second-wave financier. Banks calls himself a local insurer, but investigative journalists have shown that his insurance businesses are quite modest in size. More significant is the size of the offshore network of companies that journalists have discovered. These companies specialise in 'international contracts', 'wealth management', 'security and intelligence' and 'lobbying'. Banks manages the portfolio of niche insurance companies that he bought through this network of offshore companies. The Leave.EU campaigning company itself was set up by one of these offshore companies, called STM Fidecs, that specialised in 'maximising tax efficiencies for entrepreneurs and expatriates'. If we apply the criteria that we set out earlier, in addition to being recent, the companies from which Arron Banks extracted his wealth collect money from opaque sources (certainly not ordinary households) and invest it in opaque over-the-counter transactions. It is this that places him in second-wave finance. See Luke Harding, 'Offshore Secrets of Brexit Backer Arron Banks Revealed in Panama Papers', *Guardian*, 16 October 2016; and Leigh Baldwin and Marcus Leroux, 'Brexit's Offshore Secrets', *OpenDemocracy*, 12 April 2018.

18. See the interview excerpt in Eric Albert, 'Ces milliardaires de la City qui financent la campagne pour le Leave', *Le Monde*, 17 June 2016.

19. See François Denord and Antoine Schwartz, *L'Europe sociale n'aura pas lieu*, Paris, Raisons d'Agir, 2009; Cédric Durand (ed.), *En finir avec l'Europe*, Paris, La Fabrique, 2013; Frédéric Lordon, *La Malfaçon. Monnaie européenne et souveraineté démocratique*, Paris, Les liens qui libèrent, 2014.

20. See Albert, 'Ces milliardaires de la City'.

21. Jean-Claude Bourbon, 'L'avenir de la City paraît imprévisible après le Brexit', *La Croix*, 27 June 2016.

22. See Joseph E. Stiglitz, *Globalization and its Discontents Revisited: Anti-Globalization in the Era of Trump*, New York, W. W. Norton, 2017; see also Sara Hobolt, 'The Brexit Vote: A Divided Nation, a Divided Continent', *Journal of European Public Policy*, 9(23), pp. 1259–77, and Thomas Guénolé, *La mondialisation malheureuse*, Paris, First, 2016.

23. See Charles Wright Mills, *The Power Elite*, New York, Oxford University Press, 1956.

24. See Geoffrey Geuens, *La Finance imaginaire. Anatomie du capitalisme, des 'marches financiers' à l'oligarchie*, Brussels, Aden, 2011.

25. See Monique Pinçon-Charlot and Michel Pinçon, *Le Président des riches. Enquête sur l'oligarchie dans la France de Nicolas Sarkozy*, Paris, Zones, 2010.

26. Michel Pinçon and Monique Pinçon-Charlot, 'Inégalités entre les riches et unité de la classe bourgeoise', in Jean Lojkine, *Les Sociologies critiques du capitalisme*, Paris, PUF, 2002, p. 139.

27. David Graeber, *The Utopia of Rules: On Technology, Stupidity, and the Secret Joys of Bureaucracy*, New York, Melville House Publishing, 2015.

28. Jens Beckert, 'The "Social Order of Markets" Approach: A Reply to Kurtulus Gemici', *Theory & Society*, 41(1), 2012, p. 122.

2   Second-Wave Finance vs the European Union

1. See Marie-Claude Esposito, 'L'irrésistible ascension de la place financière de Londres dans le milieu des années 1950', *Outre-Terre*,

46, 2016, pp. 106–30; and Marie-Claude Esposito, 'Margaret Thatcher et les marchés financiers: le paradoxe de la déréglementation', *Revue française de civilisation britannique*, 14(4), 2019.

2. See Youssef Cassis, *Capitals of Capital: A History of International Financial Centres, 1780–2005*, Cambridge, Cambridge University Press, 2006, pp. 207–12.

3. See Joseph Wechsberg, 'A Prince of the City', *The New Yorker*, 1 April 1966.

4. See Niall Ferguson, *High Financier: The Lives and Time of Siegmund Warburg*, New York, Penguin, 2010, p. 94.

5. See Karl Polanyi, *The Great Transformation*, Boston, Beacon Press, 2001 [1944], pp. 8–10.

6. Denord and Schwartz, *L'Europe sociale n'aura pas lieu*, p. 54.

7. See Christopher Bellringer and Ranald Michie, 'Big Bang in the City of London: An Intentional Revolution or an Accident?', *Financial History Review*, 21(2), 2014, pp. 111–37.

8. See the excerpt from an interview with Nigel Farage's father, as reported by Henry Sanderson, 'Nigel Farage's Pinstriped Image Belies Modest City Career', *Financial Times*, 6 February 2015.

9. Ferguson, *High Financier*, p. 94.

10. See David Harvey, *A Brief History of Neoliberalism*, New York, Oxford University Press, 2005.

11. Margot Sève, *La Régulation financière face à la crise*, Brussels, Bruylant, 2013, p. 151.

12. See Megan Tobias Neely, 'Fit to Be King: How Patrimonialism on Wall Street Leads to Inequality', *Socio-Economic Review*, 16(2), pp. 365–85; see also Ken-Hou Lin and Megan Tobias Neely, *Divested: Inequality in the Age of Finance*, Oxford, Oxford University Press, 2020.

13. See Benjamin Braun, 'Asset Manager Capitalism as a Corporate Governance Regime', *SocArXiv*, 2021, https://osf.io/preprints/socarxiv/v6gue; and Benjamin Braun, 'From Exit to Control: The Structural Power of Finance under Asset Management Capitalism', *SocArXiv*, 2022, https://osf.io/preprints/socarxiv/4uesc.

14. See Leila Simona Talani, 'The Impact of the Global Financial Crisis on the City of London: Towards the End of the Hegemony?', *Competition & Change*, 15(2), 2011, pp. 12–14.

15. Philip Whyte, *Britain, Europe and the City of London: Can the Triangle Be Managed?*, Centre for European Reform Essays, 2012, p. 7.

16. See Lucia Quaglia, 'The "Old" and "New" Political Economy of Hedge Fund Regulation in the European Union', *West European Politics*, 34 (1), 2011, pp. 665–82.

17. Nikki Tait, 'Fund Managers Wary of EU vote', *Financial Times*, 6 May 2010.

18. See Dirk Schoenmaker, 'The UK Financial Sector and EU Integration after Brexit: The Issue of Passporting', in N. Campos and F. Coricelli (eds.), *The Economics of the UK–EU Relationship: From the Treaty of Rome to the Vote for Brexit*, London, Palgrave Macmillan, 2017, pp. 119–38.

19. Data on the share of the financial sector in GDP and the number of financial jobs are taken from OECD data for 2018. Sources for data on the share of the assets managed by second-wave finance are: The Investment Association (2018) for the United Kingdom; McKinsey and Preqin (2016) for the United States; and Efama and Preqin (2018) for the European Union. To build this indicator we took into account the share of the assets managed by hedge funds, private equity funds and real estate funds, the three dominant activities of second-wave finance.

20. Data on the share of the financial sector in GDP and the number of financial jobs are taken from OECD data for 2018. Sources for data on the share of the assets managed by second-wave finance are: The Investment Association (2018) for the United Kingdom; Association française de la Gestion Financière (2018) for France; PricewaterhouseCoopers (2018) for Ireland; Bundesverband Investment und Asset Management (2018) for Germany. To build this indicator we took into account the share of the assets managed by hedge funds, private equity funds and real estate funds, the three dominant activities of second-wave finance.

21. David Howarth and Lucia Quaglia, 'Brexit and the Battle for Financial Services', *Journal of European Public Policy*, 25(8), 2018, p. 1127.

22. Bundesverband Investment und Asset Management, 'Brexit. Wie kann der Fondsstandort Deutschland profitieren?', Frankfurt, BVI, 2017, p. 1.

23. See Pauline Schnapper, 'Brexit, or Theresa May's Headache', *Observatoire de la société britannique*, 21, 2018, pp. 21–34.

24. Banker quoted by Scott James and Lucia Quaglia, 'Brexit, the City and the Contingent Power of Finance', *New Political Economy*, 2019, 24(2), p. 12.

25. Geoffrey Ingham, *Capitalism Divided? The City and Industry in British Social Development*, London, Palgrave Macmillan, 1984, p. 134.

26. James and Quaglia, 'Brexit, the City and the Contingent Power of Finance', p. 12.

27. Nils Pratley, 'Crispin Odey: I Am Not Backing No-Deal Brexit as Shorting Opportunity', *Guardian*, 30 September 2019.

28. Marx, *The Eighteenth Brumaire of Louis Bonaparte*, preface to the Second Edition of 1869.

29. The two agreements were very similar. The agreement negotiated by May included an allusive reference to the principle of a 'level playing field' in competition, and the most significant contribution of Johnson's government consisted in removing this principle from the withdrawal agreement. Johnson negotiated the right to remove all references to a 'level playing field', except in the non-binding political declaration. This did not bode well for his intention to respect this principle.

30. See Oliver Shah, 'Where's Our Singapore-on-Thames? Brexit Backers Feel Let Down by High-tax PM', *The Times*, 12 September 2021.

31. See Peter Walker, 'ERG Out, CRG In: The Tory Factions Boris Johnson is Struggling to Appease', *Guardian*, 8 January 2022.

3   From European Neoliberalism to Authoritarian Libertarianism

1. See Wolfgang Streeck, *How Will Capitalism End? Essays On a Failing System*, London, Verso, 2016.

2. 'Constitutionalisation of neoliberalism' encapsulates the idea that the European construction aimed to outlaw political alternatives to neoliberalism, including social-democratic principles of government. It did so by giving a constitutional value to the 3 per cent limit on budget deficits and to rules limiting public debt to 60 per cent of GDP. Under these constitutional rules, citizens were dispossessed of the power to decide national budgets, or to modify the constraining rules, and therefore deprived of their sovereignty.

3. Jacques Sapir, 'Joffrin, l'histoire et les tyrans', *Marianne*, 24 January 2016.

4. Gavin Hewitt, 'Greece: The Dangerous Game', BBC News, 1 February 2015.

5. Frédéric Lordon, 'L'alternative de Syriza: passer sous la table ou la renverser', *Le Monde Diplomatique*, 19 January 2015.

6. Cédric Durand, 'Contre le défaitisme', in Alexis Cukier and Pierre Khalfa (eds.), *Europe, l'expérience grecque*, Paris, Editions du Croquant, 2015, p. 13.

7. Friedrich Hayek, 'The Economic Conditions of Interstate Federalism', in Friedrich Hayek (ed.), *Individualism and Economic Order*, Chicago, Chicago University Press, 1980 [1939], p. 266, quoted by Wolfgang Streeck, *Buying Time: The Delayed Crisis of Democratic Capitalism*, London, Verso, 2014.

8. Nicos Poulanztas, *Classes in Contemporary Capitalism*, London, New Left Books, 1975, p. 42.

9. See Vladimir Illich Lenin, 'Du mot d'ordre des Etats-Unis d'Europe', *Le Social-Démocrate*, 44, 23 August 1915. See also Friedrich Hayek, 'The Economic Conditions of Interstate Federalism', *New Commonwealth Quarterly*, 5(2), 1939, pp. 131–49.

10. Durand, *En finir avec l'Europe*, p. 8.

11. Denord and Schwartz, *L'Europe sociale n'aura pas lieu*, p. 47.

12. Streeck, *Buying Time*, p. 161.

13. Werner Bonefeld, 'European Integration: The Market, the Political and Class', *Capital and Class*, 26(2), 2002, p. 125.

14. Lordon, *La Malfaçon*, p. 32.

15. Lordon, *La Malfaçon*, p. 36.

16. See Durand, *Fictitious Capital*.

17. See Carl Emmerson, Paul Johnson and Ian Mitchell, 'The EU Single Market: The Value of Membership versus Access to the UK', London, Institute for Fiscal Studies, 2016, p. 18.

18. Quoted by Howard Mustoe, 'Scottish Independence: A Tale of Two Financial Centres', BBC News, 17 September 2014.

19. Lordon, *La Malfaçon*, p. 20.

20. See Brett Christophers, *Rentier Capitalism: Who Owns the Economy, and Who Pays for It*, London, Verso, 2020.

21. See Sébastien Caré, *La Pensée libertarienne. Genèse, fondements et horizons d'une utopie libérale*, Paris, PUF, 2009.

22. See Ayn Rand, *Capitalism: The Unknown Ideal*, New York, New American Library, 1966, p. 19.

23. Chris Hattingh, 'South Africa Needs a Radical Solution: Capitalism', *City Press*, 26 October 2018.

24. See Friedrich Hayek, *Denationalisation of Money*, London, Institute of Economic Affairs, 1976, and the analysis by Bruno Théret, 'Du keynésianisme au libertarianisme. La place de la monnaie dans les transformations du savoir économique autorisé', *Revue de la regulation*, 10, 2011.

25. Gilles Dostaler, 'Capitalisme et libéralisme économique', in Renaud Chartoire (ed.), *Dix questions sur le capitalisme aujourd'hui*, Paris, Sciences humaines, 2014, p. 11.

26. See Alain Supiot, *La Gouvernance par les nombres. Cours au Collège de France, 2012–2014*, Paris, Fayard, 2015.

27. See Caré, *La Pensée libertarienne*.

28. See Pascale Bourquin, Jonathan Cribb, Tom Waters and Xiaowei Xu, *Living Standards, Poverty and Inequality in the UK: 2019*, London, Institute for Fiscal Studies, 2019; and Liam Reynolds, *Homelessness in the UK: The Numbers Behind the Story*, London, Shelter, 2018.

29. See Mike Brewer and Claudia Samano Robles, 'Top Incomes in the UK: Analysis of the 2015–16 Survey of Personal Incomes', *ISER Working Paper Series*, 6, 2019.

30. See Michael Marmot, Jessica Allen, Tammy Boyce, Peter Goldblatt and Joana Morrison, *Marmot Review 10 Years On*, London, Institute of Health Equity, 2020.

31. See Emilio Casalicchio, 'Fury as Brexit Ministers "Urge Theresa May to Scrap EU Working Hours Rule"', *PoliticsHome*, 17 December 2017.

32. See for instance Streeck, *Buying Time*; Wendy Brown, Peter Gordon and Max Pensky, *Authoritarianism: Three Inquiries in Critical Theory*, Chicago, University of Chicago Press, 2018; Ugo Palheta, *La Possibilité du fascisme*, Paris, La Découverte, 2018; Chamayou, *The Ungovernable Society*; and Brown, *In the Ruins of Neoliberalism*.

33. See Palheta, *La Possibilité du fascisme*, p. 18.

34. See Bruno Latour, *Où atterrir? Comment s'orienter en politique*, Paris, La Découverte, 2017, p. 51.

35. See Karl Marx, *The Civil War in France*, London, Electric Books, 2001 [1871].

36. See Leon Trotsky, 'Again on the Question of Bonapartism: Bourgeois Bonapartism and Soviet Bonapartism', in *Writings of Leon Trotsky, Volume 7, 1934–1935*, Pathfinder Press, New York, 1971 [1935].

37. Karl Marx and Friedrich Engels, *The Communist Manifesto*, London, Verso, 2012 [1848].

38. See Jon Stone, 'Brexit: Britain Must Stay in ECHR If It Wants Trade Deal, Brussels to Insist', *The Independent*, 7 December 2017.

39. Andy Mayer, 'Protest Peacefully as Much as You Like. But Extinction Rebellion Deliberately Try to Cause Economic Damage', London, Institute of Economic Affairs, 2019.

40. See Polanyi, *The Great Transformation*.

41. Palheta, *La Possibilité du fascisme*, p. 31.

42. See Palheta, *La Possibilité du fascisme*, p. 58.

43. Pierre Bourdieu, 'The Left Hand and the Right Hand of the State', *Variant*, 32, 2008.

44. See Antonio Gramsci, *Guerre de mouvement et guerre de position*, Paris, La Fabrique, 2012.

45. Latour, *Où atterrir*, p. 10.

46. Sandrine Feydel and Christophe Bonneuil, *Prédation. Nature, le nouvel Eldorado de la finance*, Paris, La Découverte, 2015, p. 5.

47. Naomi Klein, *This Changes Everything: Capitalism vs. The Climate*, New York, Simon & Schuster, 2014, Introduction.

48. See the interview in ChatPolitics, 'Jacob Rees-Mogg on Downton Abbey, the Ukraine Crisis, and Taking Famous Women to Desert Islands', 28 March 2014, https://www.youtube.com/watch?v=nhoEwjyu6cE. Interview transcript by DeSmog in 'Jacob Rees-Mogg', *DeSmog UK*, London.

49. See Feydel and Bonneuil, *Prédation*.

50. See Philipp Golka, *Financialization as Welfare: Social Impact Investing and British Social Policy, 1997–2016*, Berlin, Springer, 2019.

51. See the publication of the British government: *Growing a Culture of Social Impact Investing in the UK*, London, HM Government, 2018.

52. David Harvey, *The New Imperialism*, Oxford, Oxford University Press, 2003, p. 168.

53. Harvey, *The New Imperialism*, p. 167.

54. Latour, *Où atterrir*, p. 30.

55. Latour, *Où atterrir*, p. 51.

Epilogue: The Drumbeat of War

1. See Bruno Amable and Stefano Palombarini, *The Last Neoliberal*, London, Verso, 2021.

2. See Alexander Ragir, 'Brazilian Hedge Funds Trounce Competition', *Washington Post*, 9 June 2011. See also Thierry Ogier, 'Sao Paulo, la "City" d'Amérique Latine', *Les Echos*, 7 August 2014.

3. See Théo Bourgeron, '"Let the Virus Spread": A Doctrine of Pandemic Management for the Libertarian-Authoritarian Capital Accumulation Regime', *Organization*, 29(3), 2022, pp. 401–13.

Index

The Pluto Press Newsletter

Hello friend of Pluto!

Want to stay on top of the best radical books
we publish?

Then sign up to be the first to hear about our
new books, as well as special events,
podcasts and videos.

You'll also get 50% off your first order with us
when you sign up.

Come and join us!

Go to bit.ly/PlutoNewsletter